25 Bicycle Tours in New Hampshire

A Guide to Selected Backcountry Roads throughout the Granite State

Tom and Susan Heavey

Revised & Expanded Edition

Backcountry Publications, Inc.   Woodstock, Vermont

Acknowledgments—We want to thank Sherri Restuccia, Wendy Ponarello and all the friendly people in New Hampshire's towns who helped us research and write this book.

An Invitation to the Reader—Although it is unlikely that the roads you cycle on these tours will change much with time, some road signs, landmarks, and other items may. If you find that changes have occurred on these routes, please let us know so we may correct them in future editions. The authors and publisher also welcome other comments and suggestions. Address all correspondence:

Editor, *Bicycle Tours*
Backcountry Publications
P.O. Box 175
Woodstock, Vermont 05091

Library of Congress Cataloging-in-Publication Data

Heavey, Tom.
  25 bicycle tours in New Hampshire.

  Rev. ed of: 20 bicycle tours in New Hampshire. 1979.
  1. Bicycle touring—New Hampshire—Guide-books.
2. New Hampshire—Description and travel—1981-
Guide-books. I. Heavey, Susan. II. Heavey, Tom.
20 bicycle tours in New Hampshire. III. Title.
IV. Title: Twenty-five bicycle tours in New Hampshire.
GV1045.5.N4H4 1985   917.42'0443   85-9069
ISBN 0-942440-25-0

Published by Backcountry Publications,
Woodstock, Vermont 05091

Photographs by the authors

Text and cover design by Richard Widhu

We wish to dedicate this book to our mother and friend,
Barbara Leedham

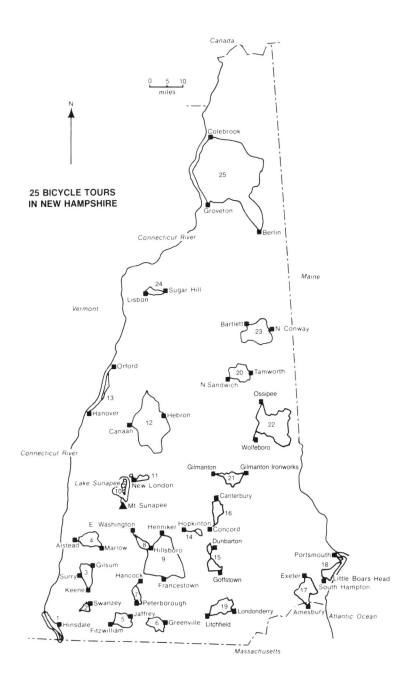

**25 BICYCLE TOURS
IN NEW HAMPSHIRE**

0   5   10
miles

Canada

Colebrook

25

Groveton

Berlin

Connecticut River

Maine

24   Sugar Hill

Lisbon

Vermont

Bartlett   23   N Conway

Orford

20   Tamworth

N Sandwich

Ossipee

13

Hanover   Hebron

Canaan   12

22

Wolfeboro

Connecticut River

Gilmanton   Gilmanton Ironworks

Lake Sunapee   11   New London

10   21

Mt Sunapee

Canterbury

16

E Washington   Henniker   Hopkinton

14   Concord

Alstead   4   Dunbarton

Marlow   8   Hillsboro

9   15   Portsmouth

Gilsum   18

Surry   3   Hancock   Goffstown   Exeter   Little Boars Head

Keene   Francestown   17   South Hampton

Swanzey   Peterborough   Amesbury   Atlantic Ocean

2   Jaffrey   19   Londonderry

1   5   6   Greenville

Hinsdale   Fitzwilliam   Litchfield

Massachusetts

Contents

Wellington State Park on Newfound Lake from a viewpoint only a short walk off your route on the Canaan-Newfound Lake tour (see tour 13).

Introduction

Bicycle tours can range from half-day trips around town to marathon cross-country journeys. Bicycle touring is an activity in which nearly everyone can participate, from grandparents to youngsters. To us, bicycle touring provides an opportunity to be outside, where the air is clean and the scenery beautiful, where the terrain provides a bit of exercise and the countryside offers attractive spots for picnicking or an occasional shop for browsing. When we search for a tour—short or long, to take with our children or by ourselves—we're looking for something that will make a day memorable.

For this guide we have put together twenty-five tours that we hope do just that. They were selected in part to bring out New Hampshire's varied beauty from the unique vantage point of the cyclist. But beyond these criteria, we sought to identify roads that are good for biking and routes of reasonable length for the average cyclist. Whatever their reasons for pedaling, cyclists, with rare exceptions, must share the roadway with motorized vehicles. And as far as we are concerned, just any road will not do. Sharing the pavement with much larger, faster-moving vehicles operated by drivers who are often unthinking and discourteous can be more an exercise in terror and survival than a rewarding personal experience. With this book we hope we can prevent the frustration and disappointment that can come when roads are randomly selected from maps.

Selecting a Tour

These loop tours have been developed from our experience with The Biking Expedition operating bicycling trips for both adults and teenagers since 1973. They range in length from fourteen miles to over one hundred miles and in difficulty from easy to challenging. Particular attention in the tour descriptions have been given to the sorts of information necessary for you to decide which trips you are capable of and will enjoy. We have attempted to remove unpleasant surprises, but not the adventure!

The tours are organized in the book roughly geographically, starting with an easy pastoral ride in the state's southwestern corner and ending with a grand trip around Coos County, north of the White Mountains. All are loops, ending where they start. At the beginning of each tour we summarize the tour distance, trip difficulty, and terrain characteristics. From this information, you should be able to decide whether a particular trip appeals to you. If it does, read on to obtain specific directions and information about lodging, points of interest, places to purchase food, and road conditions, all of which are necessary for a safe, organized, and enjoyable tour. Note that each tour direction is preceded by a cumulative mileage figure (the distance you have traveled to that point). Information about points of interest, food availability, and road conditions follows the specific tour direction.

We would like to point out that our evaluation of road conditions is not based on scientific study of road characteristics but upon our personal experience as cyclists. Five criteria are used in judging the suitability of a road for biking: apparent volume of traffic, width, presence of paved shoulders, visibility or sight distance, and condition of pavement. To us, low traffic volume is the most important factor for safe cycling; consequently, in setting up trips we attempted to keep you off major roads and on backcountry roads. While these rural lanes tend to be narrow and sometimes bumpy, lack shoulders, and have limited visibility, they usually carry very little traffic and are therefore safer. There are times when we had no choice but to use more heavily traveled routes. In these cases we point out the hazard and advise special caution — or urge you to save the route for off-season times when the volume of traffic is usually lower.

Can you do it? It may seem like a silly question to some, but to many, the thought of pedaling a bicycle for twelve, twenty, or more miles is a fearful challenge. The prospect of having a mechanical problem with the bike, or being on some deserted rural road in a state of complete exhaustion, of climbing long and painfully steep hills, of having a sore backside from that hard, narrow seat — all loom like giant roadblocks in front of many aspiring cyclists. While we do not advise the uninitiated to bite off more than they can chew, most of these fears soon disappear if you use common sense and take reasonable precautions. If you have questions about your capabilities, start with the shorter tours on less hilly terrain.

Preparing for a Tour

As in all sports, there are a few things in bicycle touring that can make the difference between a happy, fulfilling experience and a disappointing one. Before you begin touring, you should know something about bicycle touring equipment, bicycle maintenance, your physical condition, and bicycle safety.

Equipment. In general, we recommend a ten-speed bicycle for touring in New Hampshire, although a five-speed is certainly acceptable for trips in the easy and moderate categories. Unfortunately, single-speed and three-speed bikes do not offer the gear range necessary to conquer New Hampshire's inevitable hills. On the other hand, the five- and ten-speed derailleur bicycles afford tremendous mechanical advantage; once you learn to shift them efficiently so you maintain an even cadence, major barriers to both speed and hill climbing disappear. With a five- or ten-speed, most anyone can ride six miles per hour without strain, and given reasonable health and some practice, most adults can average ten to fifteen miles an hour (racing cyclists can do twenty or more miles per hour!).

For touring, a ten-speed bicycle should weigh thirty pounds or less, have good quality center pull or side pull brakes, and have a gear ratio low enough to allow for hill climbing. In the simplest terms possible, this means having twenty-six to thirty-two teeth on the largest sprocket on your freewheel and thirty-six to forty-two teeth on your smaller chainwheel. We also find that narrow seats, down-turned handlebars, and toe clips all help improve cycling efficiency, but these are not essential equipment for touring.

The kind of equipment you have does make a difference and, as with most sporting gear, you get what you pay for. In the world of bicycles, quality is generally synonymous with strong, light-weight frames; high-quality, precision-manufactured components; and careful assembly. So beware of discount specials. Today there are many moderately priced bicycles available that will perform very well on all the tours described in this book. Information about the various makes and models — and on riding techniques — is available in many publications.

Bicycle Tools and Emergency Repairs. For even a half-day tour, you should know how to make simple repairs to your bicycle. Probably the most common breakdown cyclists encounter is a flat tire. To repair it, you should have a patch kit to fix the tube, tire irons to remove the tire from the rim, and a pump to inflate the tire after the repair. If you bring along a spare tube as well, you won't have to patch the punctured one during the trip — unless you get a second flat tire. Another breakdown you should be prepared to deal with is a broken derailleur or brake cable. While this repair is not difficult, it is more time consuming and requires more tools. You need a third hand (this is the name for a tool) to hold the brakes closed, appropriate sized wrenches to loosen the nuts on the brakes or derailleur, and a pair of needle-nose pliers capable of cutting wire, since most universal brake cables have different sized nipples at either end to accommodate two types of brakes. One of the nipples has to be cut in order to thread the cable. Finally, derailleur adjustments generally require a small phillips head or narrow-headed screwdriver. You should also consider carrying a small metric tool kit and an eight-inch adjustable wrench.

In addition to the tools and spare parts mentioned, we suggest you pack the following for longer trips: a freewheel tool that fits your freewheel cluster, a chain rivet remover, a spoke wrench, spare spokes that fit your wheel, a cotterless crank tool if you have a cotterless crank or cotter pins if you have a cottered crank, spare brake blocks, a roll of electrical tape, a few spare nuts and bolts, a small can of lubricating oil, a tube of grease, and cone wrenches.

Volumes have been written about bicycle repairs and maintenance, and we urge you to purchase a small pocket-sized book to take with you if you are at all uncertain about your ability to repair your bike. Most adjustments are not difficult, even for those whose maintenance know-how normally stops with light bulb replacement. As with many other endeavors, fear of the unknown can be a major block to new experiences.

Physical Condition. Your physical condition is important to consider before taking up cycling. Obviously people vary widely when it comes to cardio-vascular efficiency, and the potential for over-extending yourself exists in cycling to the same degree that it does in other sports. Fortunately cycling, like walking, jogging, or cross-country skiing, is primarily an individual activity — one you can and should undertake at your own pace. There is little excuse for over-extending yourself, and you have only yourself to blame if you give in to the temptation to do too much too soon. Of course, if you have been physically inactive for a long period or are over thirty-five, it is probably a good idea to have a thorough physical before you begin touring. But one of the major advantages of cycling is that it is an activity in which you can participate throughout life. In addition, if proper gearing techniques are used, it is usually easier on your knees and feet than jogging is. It also has the benefit of offering the kind of moderate sustained physical involvement that helps improve cardio-vascular efficiency.

Safety. Cycling is a safe and fun activity, if you adhere to certain principles and rules of safety. One of the major problems with bicycling is that cyclists are permitted to use roadways without first obtaining a license, or otherwise demonstrating knowledge concerning the proper operation of a bicycle and rules of the road. Although New Hampshire statutes state all cyclists are "subject to and must follow all rules and regulations applicable to the operator of a motor vehicle except those rules that, by their nature, have no application," in practice anyone can ride a bicycle almost anywhere or any way he or she wants. No appointed group or organization is responsible for teaching bicycle safety, and it generally receives a low priority from enforcement agencies, with the result that people can and do ride as they please. It is little wonder, then, that accidents involving bikes are not uncommon.

But it does not have to be that way, especially if you adhere to the following guidelines: BE ALERT, BE VISIBLE, and BE PREDICTABLE. You must be ALERT because you cannot depend upon a motorist to look out for your welfare; you must be ready to take evasive action if necessary. Common examples of this type of situation include: a motorist making a right turn after passing a cyclist causing the cyclist to ride into the side of the turning vehicle; a motorist making a left turn at an intersection into the path of an oncoming cyclist; and a motorist in a parked vehicle opening a door into the path of the oncoming cyclist or pulling out from a parking place without yielding to the cyclist.

You must be VISIBLE in order to give the motorist every opportunity to see you. Most drivers are courteous if they see you, but they are not generally looking for cyclists. Rather, they are looking for other cars and trucks, which pose more personal danger to them than do cyclists. It should come as no surprise that, according to a recent study, a large percentage of fatal cycling accidents occur at night when visibility is reduced. Three things a cyclist can do to enhance visibility are to wear bright clothing, use bicycle flags, and NEVER ride at night.

Your movements on your bicycle should be PREDICTABLE. Many bicycle accidents occur when cyclists make sudden turns or move into the path of a vehicle without allowing the driver sufficient time to take evasive action. Examples of such situations include: a cyclist riding from a midblock location into traffic; a cyclist riding into cross traffic from an intersection controlled by a stop sign or traffic signal; and a cyclist riding along the right side of a street and then suddenly veering left into the path of a car.

In addition to being alert, visible, and predictable, there are some other specific actions you can take to protect yourself while cycling. The most important is to WEAR A HELMET. Your head is the most vulnerable part of your body, and a good quality helmet, such as the Bell Helmet or the MSR, can make the difference should you fall. Another important precau-

You don't need to be an experienced mechanic to make some of the more basic repairs to your bicycle.

tion is to stay in control on downgrades. It is easy to forget that a bicycle can reach speeds of forty-five to fifty-five miles per hour on steep downgrades. At those speeds, it does not take a very large obstacle such as a rock, pothole, or patch of sand to throw you out of control.

Finally, a few common sense bike riding rules are: ride in a straight line, never zigzag; ride in single file, always with traffic, never against it; listen for approaching traffic that you may not yet see; keep enough space between you and the bike in front of you to allow for an emergency stop; be alert for road hazards such as potholes, loose gravel and sand, parallel storm grates, expansion joints on bridges, and especially railroad crossings, where tracks can easily throw you out of control. And always practice defensive cycling.

Remember, on the tours outlined in this book you are often on back-country New Hampshire roads where the scenery is beautiful and the traffic very light. In such settings, it is easy to be lulled into a sense of security and safety. But always be alert for an unexpected vehicle coming over the top of the hill or around the next bend, because the driver is probably not expecting you either.

Cycling is fun, healthful, and refreshing. Get involved, and may you have a long hill down and a stiff tailwind!

Monadnock Region

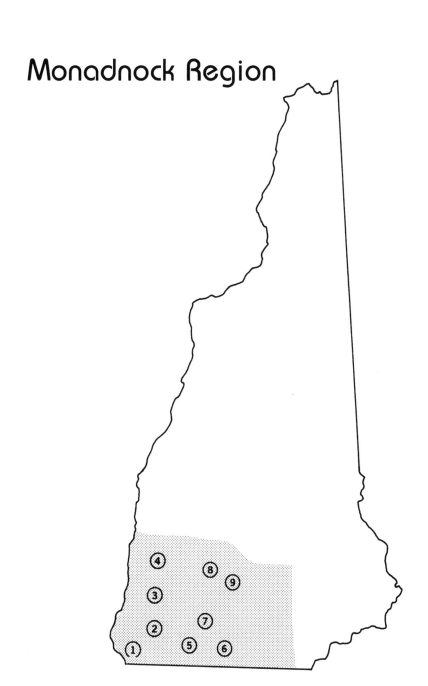

1
Tri-Stater

25.8 miles; easy to moderate cycling
Level to rolling terrain

While this is a book about bicycle touring in New Hampshire, in the interest of safety and good touring, we have bent the ground rules somewhat for this loop through the fertile farmland of the Connecticut River Valley. Our Tri-Stater starts in the southwestern part of the Granite State, crosses into Northfield, Massachusetts, and winds back through Vernon and Brattleboro, Vermont. If you have successfully completed one of the easy, half-day trips or wish to impress your friends with your superb physical and athletic ability by cycling in three states in one day, this is the trip for you. Actually, it is a great trip for anyone who can appreciate the majestic beauty of the Connecticut River and the serenity of country roads that twist and wind to open up new scenes around every bend.

There are numerous motels where you can find lodging in Brattleboro. For a special treat you might try the Chesterfield Inn (256-3211) located on NH 9 in Chesterfield, New Hampshire, 1.6 miles east of the Vermont border. Recently renovated, this big old colonial was until recently an antique carriage and sleigh museum. With beautiful views of the Vermont hills and Connecticut River Valley to the west, it has lovely rooms, several of which contain fireplaces and whirlpools. In Northfield, Massachusetts you can stay at Centennial House Bed and Breakfast (413-498-5921) located on MA 10/MA 63 across from the Northfield Fire Station 0.9 mile south of Northfield Pizza House.

The tour begins at a wayside rest area on NH 119, about 1 mile south of the Hinsdale Raceway. Developed by Boy Scout Troop 307 in a shady pine grove next to the Connecticut River, it offers sufficient room to park your car. It is easy to miss this spot however. Look for a small rest area sign (a pine tree symbol with an arrow) just before the unpaved turn into the pine grove.

0.0   From the rest area, head east on NH 119 toward the center of Hinsdale for 2.7 miles to NH 63, on your right.

On your way into Hinsdale you pass several other small wayside picnic areas with great views of the Connecticut River.

Several food stores line the stretch of NH 119 between the rest area and the raceway. Johnny's Drive-in at the junction of NH 119 and NH 63 in Hinsdale is open everyday.

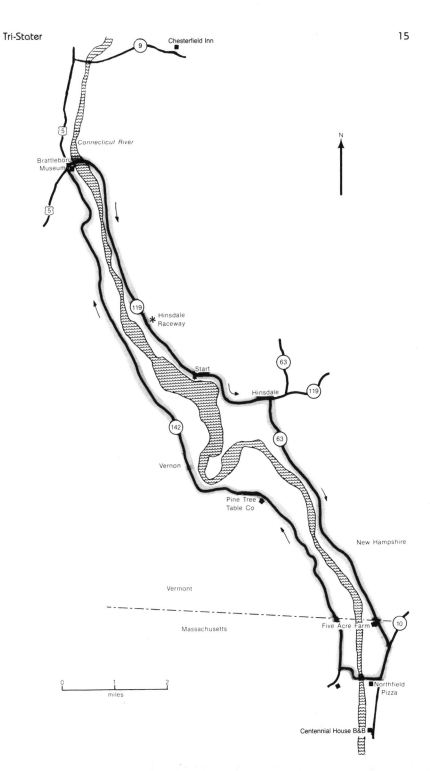

Many productive, working farms dot the rolling countryside of the Connecticut River Valley.

NH 119 in this area has a good surface but no shoulder except for a 0.4-mile section at the trip's beginning. The terrain here is rolling with several short, moderately steep upgrades. Traffic is generally light to moderate.

2.7 Turn right onto NH 63 and ride south for 5.5 miles. You cross the state border into Northfield, Massachusetts, just before reaching MA 10.

A great road for cycling, NH 63 twists, dips, and turns as it hugs the eastern edge of the Connecticut River Valley. High enough to provide long views of corn fields and grazing cattle, yet without mind-blowing hills to challenge your legs and heart, it is a delight to ride. A small picnic area on the right 3.2 miles from the NH 19/NH 63 junction, offers a nice spot to bask in the sun and enjoy the scenery. Five Acre Farm, located 0.5 mile before you reach MA 10, sells fresh vegetables during the summer. Pauchaug Brook Fish and Wildlife Management Area, operated by the Massachusetts Division of Fisheries and Wildlife, is located at the junction of the two highways.

NH 63 is narrow with no shoulders but a smooth surface. Visibility is generally good except at an occasional sharp turn or sudden dip. Traffic tends to be light.

8.2 At the intersection, turn right onto MA 10/MA 63 and ride 0.6 mile to an unmarked road on the right, just before the Northfield Pizza House.

Northfield-Mount Hermon School, a coeducational boarding school, is set high above the Connecticut River adjacent to MA 10/MA 63 on the northeast side of Northfield.

In addition to the Pizza House, there are several stores and restaurants in Northfield on MA 10/Ma 63. Northfield Country Store, 1.1 miles south of our turnoff, is open daily 8–8. The IGA directly across the street is also open all day everyday. Murray's Country Kitchen, adjacent to the IGA is a small restaurant from which you can observe the gracious main street of Northfield with its beautifully kept houses and manicured lawns.

The Bicycle Barn, located 1.2 miles south of the Pizza House, is open 9–5 Mon.–Sat., should you need parts or repairs.

MA 10/MA 63 is a wide, two-lane road with a smooth surface. While it is a major route with some truck traffic, this short section that leads into town is generally safe to travel because the speed limit is low.

8.8 By the Northfield Pizza House, turn right onto the unmarked road, and prepare yourself for a rapid, twisting descent to a bridge over the Connecticut River. After crossing the river, the road makes a sharp right and then a sharp left over a railroad bridge before meeting VT 142, 1.6 miles from MA 10/MA 63.

Note that the first bridge has a very rough surface so slow down before you cross it or you may damage your wheels. This second bridge is surfaced with wood planks going parallel with your wheels. Be careful as it is easy to fall.

If you turn left (south) when you reach VT 142 and ride for 0.1 mile, you come to a general store, where you can purchase provisions. Initially, the unmarked road connecting MA 10/MA 63 with VT 142 is narrow, steep, and twisting and requires caution. However, on the west side of the river it is quite level with good visibility.

10.4 At the intersection, turn right and head north on VT 142 for 11.2 miles to VT 119 in Brattleboro.

3 miles from where you turn onto VT 142 you come to School House Grocery on the right (7:30–9 daily). Though small, it is well stocked and even has a deli.

Much like NH 63 on the other side of the Connecticut River, this route offers easy cycling through prosperous farm country with occasional views of the river. Pine Tree Table Company's factory store, located on the left in 3.4 miles, is open seven days a week. Two historical markers, one for Vernon's First Meeting House and the other for the tomb of Jemima Tute (1723–1805), famed "fair captive," are located at 4.3 miles and 6.2 miles respectively. The Brattleboro Museum and Art Center, located at the junction of VT 142 and US 5 in Brattleboro is open Tuesday–Friday noon–4; Saturday and Sunday 1–4.

Brattleboro is a large enough town to support many restaurants and food stores.

VT 142 is a smooth, narrow, two-lane road with no shoulders and light traffic. Visibility is generally good except for a few areas where curves and grades limit sight distance. For the most part the terrain is quite flat, though there are a few rolling hills. You should be alert for several railroad crossings, especially near Brattleboro.

21.6 At the intersection, turn right toward New Hampshire, head down a short hill (beware of the railroad tracks at the bottom!), and cross the Connecticut River (be careful on the slippery iron grate bridge).

Note that there is a pedestrian walkway to the left side of this bridge if you wish to avoid the metal grating. As you cross, the road becomes NH 119. Continue for 4.2 miles to your car — and a soft seat.

NH 119 is a wide road with good visibility. Initially the shoulder is of poor quality but later widens to a smooth paved surface as you near Hinsdale Race Track. Traffic is generally light to moderate except during racing times at Hinsdale Raceway, when it can be heavy. There is one short, steep hill to climb soon after you cross the bridge over the Connecticut.

25.8 You made it! You are back at the rest area where you began your trip.

2

Swanzey Covered Bridges

15.2 miles; easy cycling
Level to rolling terrain

Covered bridges are as characteristic of New Hampshire as maple syrup, baked beans, and church suppers. Their presence yields a comforting sense of permanence and continuity with the past, as well as a release from the plastic and glitter of twentieth-century life. Swanzey, in the southwest corner of the state, is proud possessor of four such spans, all conveniently connected by a network of gently rolling country roads. On this route, an excellent beginning trip for both adults and children, you experience a kinship with early farmers and settlers, who like you, traveled these byways over the same bridges in nonmotorized fashion.

When you reach these relics, take a moment to examine how they are put together. Because covered bridges were originally built to carry loaded haywagons over rivers and thus were designed and constructed by local farmers, each has its own character. The roof and siding that cover the bridge (which had to be high enough to accommodate the loaded wagons) were meant primarily to safeguard the truss work, not passersby, from the elements.

Overnight accommodations can be found in the city of Keene, three miles to the north. See our Surry Mountain–Gilsum Tour for some suggestions.

A convenient starting point for this trip is at the junction of NH 32 and Sawyers Crossing Road, in the center of Swanzey. Monadnock Regional High School and Swanzey Town Hall, both adjacent to this intersection, have parking lots where you can leave your car.

0.0 From the high school or town hall in Swanzey, head south on NH 32 for 1.5 miles to Carlton Road.

NH 32 is a two-lane road with no shoulder, a smooth surface, good visibility, and low traffic. The terrain is mostly level.

1.5 At Carlton Road, turn left and travel 1.1 miles, passing through your first covered bridge, to the junction of Carlton Road and Webber Hill Road (note the white, two-chimney colonial on the left at this T-intersection).

The Carlton covered bridge, which spans South Brook, is thought to be one of the oldest covered bridges in the area. It is constructed in the Queenpost truss style, a design used on the earliest bridges that farmers built employing the same methods they used for their churches and barns. Although once quite common, few bridges that were constructed in this style are standing today.

Carlton Road is quite level, except for one moderate upgrade just beyond the bridge. It is narrow and has no shoulder, little traffic, and an acceptable surface for cycling.

2.6 Turn right on Webber Hill Road, head downhill past the East Swanzey Post Office, and then bear right as you merge with another unmarked road. A biker's delight with a smooth, level surface, this road brings you back to NH 32 in 1 mile.

The back roads in this area are all much alike. They tend to be narrow with no shoulder, have reasonably smooth surfaces with occasional frost heaves, and pass over slightly rolling terrain.

3.6 At the intersection, bear right on NH 32, riding north for 0.2 mile to Swanzey Lake Road, on the left.

3.8 Turn left onto Swanzey Lake Road, which you follow for 3.9 miles to a T-junction with an unmarked road.

If you are looking for a place to go swimming, bear right off Swanzey

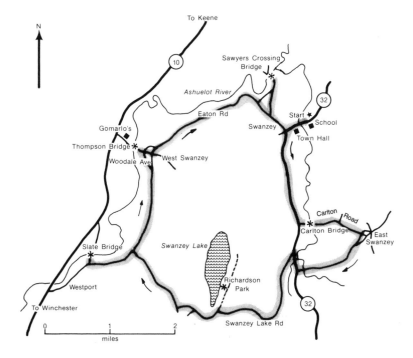

Lake Road onto the road that rings Swanzey Lake. In about 0.3 mile you'll come to Richardson Park, which offers swimming and picnicking for a small admission charge.

Swanzey Lake Road is similar to the other backcountry roads you travel on this tour. It has a number of twists and turns, but if you stay on the surfaced road, you should not get lost.

7.7   At the T-junction, turn left on the Westport Road (unmarked) heading toward Westport and Winchester (beware of railroad tracks a short distance along this road), and ride 0.7 mile to a stop sign.

8.4   At the stop sign, turn right toward Keene, and ride 0.1 mile to the Slate covered bridge.

The Slate covered bridge stretches 142½ feet across the Ashuelot River. Built in 1862, this bridge replaced another that had been erected in the same spot in 1800.

8.5   Retrace your route 0.1 mile to Westport Road, turn left and ride for another 2.2 miles to a four-way stop sign at the junction of High Street and Homestead Road. Be aware that the road names in this area change frequently and can cause confusion. The name of Westport Road (unmarked) changes to Homestead Road as you approach West Swanzey. A landmark

The Thompson Bridge still has one of its two sidewalks.

to look for to be sure you are headed in the right direction is Holbrook Home Boarding House on the left 0.2 mile before the junction of High Street and Homestead Road.

10.8 Turn left on High Street and ride 0.2 mile to Thompson covered bridge. This bridge, which also spans the Ashuelot River, originally had two sidewalks and still has one today.

For refreshments, stop at Gomarlo's Inc., on the west side of the Thompson covered bridge. This store is open all day, every day. Nick's Restaurant is located just beyond Gomarlo's and is open 8–7 Mon.–Sat.

11.0 Retrace your route 0.2 mile to the four-way stop sign and turn left. As you turn left this road is marked as Railroad Street but soon merges with Eaton Road. Follow this road for 2.4 miles to Sawyers Crossing Road.

13.6 Turn left onto Sawyer Crossing Road and ride 0.6 mile to the last and longest covered bridge on this tour.

The Sawyers Crossing covered bridge, like the Thompson and Slate bridges, is an example of Town lattice truss construction. This type of covered bridge design was developed in the early 1830s by Ithiel Town, a great engineer of his time.

14.2 Retrace your route to the junction of Eaton Road and Sawyers Crossing Road. Bear left (still named Sawyers Crossing Road) and ride 0.4 mile back to the junction of NH 32.

15.2 You are back at the intersection of NH 32 and Sawyers Crossing Road where you began the tour.

3

Surry Mountain-Gilsum

22.3 miles; moderate to challenging cycling
Rolling to hilly terrain, one major hill

Because it offers lots of variety, our trip around Surry Mountain, just north of Keene, can be approached in a number of ways. It is ideal for cyclists who seek the solitude of an early morning ride along the Ashuelot River, the challenge of a steep hill near Gilsum, and the exhilaration of a long descent to the city of Keene. Those who wish a full day's outing have their choice of any number of activities to break up the cycling: a stop in Keene, an active college town, is the perfect counterpoint to a trip through the countryside; the Surry Mountain Recreation Area, whose dam and reservoir were built as a flood-control project by the Army Corps of Engineers in 1941, offers outdoor activities from swimming to camping; and Gilsum, the site of some sixty inactive mines which a century ago produced beryl, rose quartz, and even gold, is an enticing detour.

The city of Keene has a number of motels and inns including: Best Western Valley Green Motel, 379 West Street (352-7350), Winding Brook Lodge, Park Avenue (352-3111), and the Ramada Inn at the junction of NH 10 and NH 101 (357-3038). For more home-like accommodations, try the Carriage Barn Guest House (357-3812) on Main Street across from the campus of Keene State College.

The trip begins at Surry Mountain Recreation Area on NH 12A, 5.5 miles north of Central Square in Keene. Do not follow Dam Road, which leads to the dam and office building. Continue 1.1 miles past this road to the entrance of the day-use area, on the right, where a large parking lot, changing house, beach, picnic tables, and well-maintained grounds are located. The parking lot can be used from the beginning of May until the end of September only; it is flooded during the remaining months.

0.0 From the parking lot, return to NH 12A and turn right, heading north for 3.8 miles to Gilsum Road, on your right.

Surry Mountain Recreation Area offers swimming, boating, hiking, picnicking, fishing, and camping. The village of Surry is located 1.1 miles north of the recreation area entrance, off NH 12A on Crain Road.

NH 12A has a smooth surface and good visibility, but no shoulder. The terrain is flat to rolling. Traffic tends to be light but picks up during commuting hours.

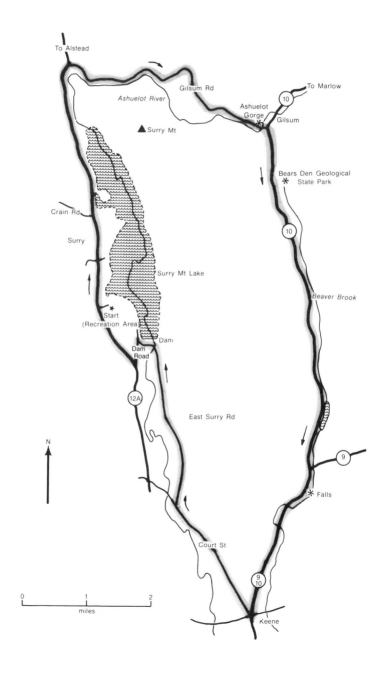

To Alstead

Gilsum Rd

Ashuelot River

To Marlow

10

Ashuelot
Gorge

Gilsum

▲ Surry Mt

Bears Den Geological
State Park

Crain Rd

10

Surry

Beaver Brook

Surry Mt Lake

Start
(Recreation Area)

Dam

Dam
Road

12A

East Surry Rd

N

9

Falls

Court St

9
10

0   1   2
miles

Keene

3.8   Turn right onto Gilsum road and proceed for 4.2 miles to NH 10.

Here you wind alongside the Ashuelot River through a small valley where the vegetation varies from thick forest to open meadow. Ashuelot Gorge, at the junction of Gilsum Road and NH 10, is worth a look from the stone arch bridge that spans it. If you turn left on NH 10 and ride toward Gilsum, you can take advantage of a swimming area to your left on the Ashuelot River. Should you wish to explore old mines or dig for semi-precious stones, stop at the Gilsum Village Store established 1881, (open all day every day and has a small deli) or write to the Gilsum Library (Box 57, Gilsum, NH 03448) for a copy of an area map ($.25). If your timing is right, you can attend Gilsum's annual Rock Swap, held during the last week of June. During the Swap, hundreds of rockhounds trade, dig, and buy various types of semi-precious stones.

The two-lane Gilsum Road is narrow, with no shoulder and a moderately bumpy surface. Because of its many twists and turns, visibility is limited; however, traffic is light. The terrain is moderately hilly, with a very gradual rise as you proceed upstream along the Ashuelot. A steep 0.3-mile downgrade with a sharp turn awaits you 3 miles after turning on Gilsum Road. Caution is advised.

8.0   Turn right onto NH 10 and immediately begin a steep 0.8-mile climb, the trip's most difficult, and continue for a total of 5.3 miles to the junction of NH 10 and NH 9.

NH 10, a major north/south highway, has a smooth surface, adequate width, and generally good visibility.

There is an intermittent shoulder soon after you turn onto this route which turns to a nicely paved, full-lane shoulder as you approach Keene.

With the exception of the steep hill immediately south of Gilsum Road, the terrain is either level or slopes down towards Keene. There are some trucks, but except for peak periods on weekends, traffic conditions are usually acceptable. While this road is not generally recommended for young children or very inexperienced cyclists, most people should have no major difficulty here.

13.3   At the junction of NH 10 and NH 9, turn right and ride 0.7 mille to the Washington Street exit. Follow the exit for 0.4 mile to a stop sign. Cross NH 9/NH 10 and continue for 1.6 miles to Central Square in Keene.

When you turn right into NH 9/NH 10, you will be on a new section of divided, four-lane highway with no shoulder for a short distance. The visibility is quite good here and you should be able to ride with little difficulty. You will immediately begin to ascend for 0.5 mile to a crest where the road narrows down to two lanes with a wide paved shoulder. Caution: as you begin to descend the hill and exit onto Washington Street, there are several storm sewers with parallel grates that could cause a nasty fall if your wheel is caught in one.

15.9   When you reach Keene, proceed approximately one-quarter of the way around Central Square, turn sharply right onto Court Street (also NH 12A) near the Keene Food Mart, and continue on Court Street for 2.1 miles to East Surry Road (note the sign for Bretwood Golf Course).

Many fine colonial and Victorian homes line the streets around Central Square. Keene State College, Thorne Art Gallery, and Wyman Tavern are but a few of the many attractions in this community.

Brando's Deli on Washington Street across from the Junior High School makes great sandwiches (6–6 Mon.–Fri., 7–5 Sat.).

Keene has many fine restaurants. We recommend Peter Christian's Tavern, Main Street, serving stews, soups, quiches and more (11:30–12:30, 357-3100); and Henry David's, 81 Main Street, with great decor and equally fine food (11:30–1 daily, 352-0608).

There are also numerous food stores in Keene should you wish to purchase lunch or snacks.

Court street has moderate to heavy traffic. For 0.8 mile, its wide shoulder is also used for parking, so be alert for people opening car

From a bicycle you have an opportunity to enjoy many scenes which often escape the motorist.

doors in your path. The road is reasonably flat, and a sidewalk exists all the way to East Surry Road.

18.0   At East Surry Road, bear right and ride for 2.8 miles to Dam Road.
East Surry Road has a smooth surface, no shoulder, and low traffic. Note that the road makes a sharp left turn and goes over a small bridge beyond the golf course. Just stay on the paved road.

20.8   At Dam Road, turn left and ride for 0.4 mile to NH 12A.
Dam Road also has a smooth surface, no shoulder, and little traffic.

21.2   At the junction of NH 12A, turn right and cycle 1.1 miles back to the Surry Mountain Recreation Area.

22.3   You are at the entrance to the day-use area and the end of your trip.

4

Alstead-Marlow

25.1 miles; challenging cycling
Level to hilly terrain

Alstead, Marlow, and South Acworth: vintage New Hampshire at its best! Here there are no resorts or suburban developments, only tree-shaded lanes along mountain brooks that tumble and roll on their way to the Connecticut River and individualists whose spirit and fortitude are infectious. Here you sense that life is neither hurried nor complicated. While some bicycle tours should be approached as an experience in solitude, this is not one of those; the residents of these towns seem more than willing to share themselves and their experiences with you, and you should enjoy them. A retired printer turned rockhound and a young cabinet maker who always has a pot of coffee on the stove are some of the people who can make this trip more than just a day's ride.

Because you are touring rugged land that rises upward and eastward from the Connecticut River Valley, this tour is not particularly easy. In fact, fully one-third of the route, about eight miles, involves a climb, some of it steep. But the other two-thirds is either flat or downhill. It's not a bad ratio, especially as you do the climbing early in the trip. Your efforts are rewarded by outstanding scenery and about sixteen miles of effortless biking.

While there is no lodging available on the route described below, we suggest you try the Stoddard Inn on NH 123, six miles southeast of Marlow. Opened by John and Jenifer Parkinson in September, 1983 in an 1830s colonial, this small but elegant inn offers quality dining and accommodations in an idlyic New England setting (446-7873).

The tour begins in the village of Alstead, located on NH 12A/NH 123, approximately twenty-five miles north of Keene. Main Street, which is the numbered highway, offers ample opportunity for on-street parking. There is also space at the Shedd Porter Memorial Library at the village's west end; however, we suggest that you check with the librarian before parking there.

0.0   Begin by traveling east on Main Street (NH 12A/NH 123) past the stores and school for 0.7 mile to the junction with NH 123A.

The Village Store (7–9 Mon.–Sat.; 8–9 Sun.), on Alstead's Main Street, is the only grocery store where you can buy food until you reach NH 10 in Marlow, about ten miles into your tour. Check the village bulletin board next to the entrance for local events of interest.

NH 12A/NH 123 has a smooth surface, two wide lanes, very little shoulder, and light to moderate traffic.

0.7   At the junction, take the right fork and continue on NH 12A/NH 123 toward Keene for another 0.7 mile, were the road forks again.

1.4   At the fork, stay left on NH 123 where NH 12A heads south to Keene. Continue on this road through Mill Hollow and East Alstead for 8.3 miles to NH 10 in Marlow.

This stretch offers numerous views of farmland set against mountains. Mill Hollow, a late-eighteenth-century community of small, individually operated mills, still has a standing grist mill. East Alstead is a hilltop town with well-kept homes and a fantastic view of Lake Warren to the southwest. Four miles beyond East Alstead you pass beneath the Marlow Profile, a rocky cliff that bears a close resemblance to New Hampshire's symbol of the Great Stone Face.

Breshear's Farm Stand is located 1.2 miles from Alstead on the right side of NH 123.

Just before the village of Marlow, look for the Peace Barn on the right, an antique shop specializing in primitive country pine.

After NH 12A splits off toward Keene, NH 123 narrows and the shoulder disappears completely. However, the visibility is good and there is little traffic. You climb nearly the entire 8.3 miles to Marlow. For the most part the slope is gradual, but there are occasional steep pitches, which are sometimes relieved by a level stretch or downgrade.

9.7   At the junction of NH 123 and NH 10 in Marlow, turn left on NH 10 and ride north for 4.5 miles to NH 123A, on your left.

In the center of Marlow, named after famed playwright and author Christopher Marlowe, the grounds around a lily pond offer a pleasant rest stop. The Ashuelot River and Stone Pond are located along your route.

The Marlow Grocery (8–7 daily) is located at the junction of NH 123 and NH 10.

NH 10 provides a smooth surface for biking. While it has only an intermittent shoulder and moderate traffic, including some trucks, the visibility is good and the terrain quite flat, resulting in easy, enjoyable cycling.

14.2   At the junction, turn left and follow NH 123A for 10.2 miles downhill through South Acworth to NH 12A/NH 123, back into Alstead.

The Cold River, a shallow, rocky stream paralleling the road, offers frequent opportunities for a refreshing wade. Harvey Bailey's Beryl Mountain Mineral Shop is located 1 mile off your route but is well worth the extra 2 miles cycling to visit. Watch for a sign saying "Mineral Shop" on a bridge to your left 2.4 miles beyond the tiny hamlet of South Acworth. The sign is easy to miss, so for reference look for Green Mountain Farm across the road from the bridge. The sign points left to an unmarked road, which you follow 1 mile over a smooth surface and flat terrain to the shop. Open "eight days a week," it contains a large collection of mica, rose quartz, garnet, pyrite, and other minerals collected from abandoned mines in the area. However beautiful the stones, it is really the genial Mr. Bailey who makes the trip worthwhile. A retired printer, he freely shares his extensive knowledge of the history and location of New Hampshire mineral sites with anyone who asks.

Beyond the cutoff to the mineral shop you pass the Langdon–Cold River covered bridge, a seventy-eight-foot span built in 1869 by Albert Granger. Just before you reach NH 12A/NH 123 again you coast past Villas Pool (11–7), a popular swimming and picnic area that offers swan boat rides in the summer.

In South Acworth the Village Store, founded in 1865, is open Monday through Saturday 7–7, Sunday, 10–7.

The first 2.1 miles on NH 123A descend steeply alongside a tree-shaded brook. On a sunny day the lacy shadows make it difficult to see the bumps and cracks in the road. Be forewarned that the road turns sharply left at the bottom of this steep stretch. The remaining miles to Alstead slope less steeply downward. The road is narrow and winding and has a rough but very ridable surface. There is no shoulder.

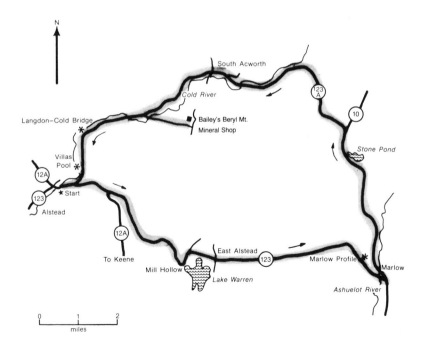

The Cold River and its quiet undisturbed banks offer a refreshing rest stop on the Alstead-Marlow tour.

24.4   At the junction turn right onto NH 12A/NH 123 to retrace the last 0.7 mile to the village of Alstead.

25.1   You are back where you started.

If you have time continue past the library and over the bridge to Entrance's, Inc. Donald Pecora, the young proprietor, may treat you to a cup of coffee as he demonstrates how he handcrafts the beautiful woodwork, furniture and toys for which he has gained a considerable reputation.

5

Jaffrey-Fitzwilliam

20.2 miles; moderate cycling
Rolling terrain, some short, steep hills

Mount Monadnock, rising nearly 2,000 feet above surrounding hills to a peak of 3,165 feet, is the most dominant land feature in southwestern New Hampshire. Tucked in its shadow are the towns of Jaffrey and Fitzwilliam, whose rolling terrain and secondary roads offer fine opportunities for bicycle touring. Since this tour is relatively short and only moderately demanding, it can easily be combined with stops at historic sites and antique shops or a side trip up Mount Monadnock if you have a full day to spend in the area.

Two lovely inns that provide food and lodging are the Fitzwilliam Inn (585-9000) in Fitzwilliam and the Woodbound Inn (532-8341), Woodbound Road in Jaffrey. Directions to both can be found by following the tour route which goes by both establishments.

Begin your trip in Jaffrey at the junction of US 202, NH 137, and NH 124. Ample parking can be found along the main street and in the municipal parking lot.

0.0 From Jaffrey, head west on NH 124 for 4.4 miles through Jaffrey Center to Fitzwilliam Road, on your left. There's a red farmhouse on your right at this turn.

The Jaffrey Civic Center on the right side of NH 124 just west of the US 202/NH 137 junction, is the place to pick up information about the area's fascinating history and people. They include Willa Cather, the Pulitzer-prize-winning writer who is buried in Jaffrey Center; Amos Fortune, a negro slave who purchased his freedom in Massachusetts at the age of fifty-nine and then moved to Jaffrey in 1781 where he established a tannery an lived as a highly respected citizen until his death in 1801; and Hannah Davis, a spinster left destitute at the age of thirty-four who supported herself by manufacturing wooden hat boxes, which have since become collector's items.

The Civic Center is open Monday through Saturday 1:30–5 (532-6527 or 532-8811). In Jaffrey Center, which you pass through in 1.6 miles, there are several historic homes and buildings, including the Old Meeting House, First Church, Amos Fortune's grave, and The Little Red Schoolhouse.

If you would like to learn a bit about the area's natural history, watch for the signs to Monadnock State Park 0.5 mile beyond Jaffrey Center. The road leads 2 miles into the park to Monadnock Ecocenter, an education and information center operated by the Society of the Protection of New Hampshire Forests at the trailhead of the White Dot Trail that leads up the famous mountain.

There are several stores and restaurants in Jaffrey, the last place to buy food until you reach Fitzwilliam. Norm's Thriftway (7:30–9 daily) is on US 202 just north of its junction with NH 124.

From Jaffrey to Jaffrey Center, NH 124 has a smooth surface and a two-foot-wide paved shoulder. Visibility is good, the terrain gentle, and the traffic moderate. As you leave Jaffrey Center, the road narrows and the shoulder disappears. The surface remains smooth, though.

4.4   At Fitzwilliam Road, turn left and follow this road 4 miles to its junction with NH 12 in Fitzwilliam. Note that Old Fitzwilliam Road joins Fitzwilliam Road from the left after 0.9 mile. Do not go left on Old Fitzwilliam Road. Follow Fitzwilliam Road for 0.2 mile beyond this junction where the road again forks. Old Country Road goes to the right; you stay left on Fitzwilliam Road.

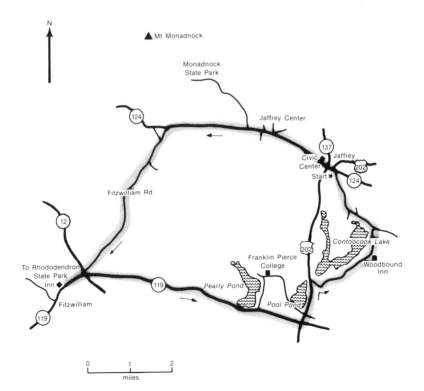

Fitzwilliam Road is a narrow backcountry road with a reasonably smooth surface, no shoulder, good visibility, and very little traffic.

8.4 At this intersection, ride directly across NH 12 and immediately join NH 119 in Fitzwilliam. Turn right on NH 119 and follow NH 119 a short distance to the village green, circle it and then retrace your route to the junction of NH 12 and NH 119.

In Fitzwilliam there are a number of antique shops worth visiting. The Fitzwilliam Inn on the common has been offering passersby lodging, food, and good cheer since 1796. The Meeting House and Blake House, two more historical buildings on the green, are also worth noting. For a side trip, you may wish to ride 2.6 miles northwest of the Fitzwilliam green to Rhododendron State Park. Encompassing sixteen acres of wild rhododendrons, it's one of the largest tracts of this species north of the Allegheny Mountains. While your efforts as a cyclist to reach the park are hindered by a bumpy, hilly road, it is well worth a visit in mid-July when the blossoms are at their peak.

Roy's Market (9–6:30 Mon.–Sat., 10–1 Sun.) is on NH 119 just before the Fitzwilliam Green. It has a deli where you can purchase coldcuts. The Fitzwilliam Inn serves lunch noon–2 and dinner 6–9:30 daily.

NH 12 and NH 119 through Fitzwilliam are narrow, with moderately heavy but slow-moving traffic.

9.2 From the junction, proceed east toward West Rindge along NH 119 for 5.5 miles to the junction with US 202.

Franklin Pierce College, on your left 4 miles east of Fitzwilliam, is a four-year, liberal arts school that was founded in 1962. It enrolls over seven hundred students.

There is a Citgo Station with a convenience store located at the junction of NH 119 and US 202 in West Rindge. It is open all day every day.

NH 119, here wide with a good surface but no shoulder, leads you over rolling terrain. It generally carries moderately heavy traffic, but the visibility is excellent.

14.7 At West Rindge, turn left onto US 202 and follow it north 1 mile past Poole Pond (on your left) to an unmarked road on your right just beyond a sign for Woodmere Campground and Woodbound Inn.

Old Forge Restaurant (noon–3, 5–9 Tues.–Sat.; noon–8 Sun.) is located on US 202 0.3 mile from its junction with NH 119 and features country cooking.

US 202 is wider than NH 119 and has paved a shoulder eight feet wide that is suitable for biking. While US 202 is a major route, its wide shoulder and excellent visibility make it very safe for cycling.

15.7 Beyond the sign for the campground, turn right onto Woodbound Road (unmarked) and follow it for 0.3 mile.

Once you leave US 202, the roads back to Jaffrey are all typical rural New Hampshire lanes. Winding over rolling terrain, they have bumpy surfaces, no shoulders, and only fair visibility, but what little traffic they carry travels slowly.

16.0 At the fork, turn sharply left and continue 2.4 miles past the golf course and the Woodbound Inn to a stop sign at a T-junction.

The Woodbound Inn, a forty-room inn/resort on Contoocook Lake just outside the Jaffrey town line, offers a wide variety of summer and winter sports, including a par three golf course which is open to the public.

The beach on Contoocook Lake is maintained by the town of Jaffrey and is open to the public.

18.4 At the stop sign, turn left onto Squantum Road (unmarked), ride past the beach at Contoocook Lake, and continue for 0.3 mile to the junction of this road with Howard Hill Road. Bear right and ride 0.2 mile to a stop sign. Continue straight ahead for 0.5 mile to another stop sign. Turn right and ride 0.6 mile to a stop sign and blinking red light in downtown Jaffrey. Go straight ahead for 0.2 mile to your starting point at the junction of this road with US 202 and NH 137.

20.2 You are back on NH 124 in Jaffrey, where you began this trip.

If you maintain an even cadence, the rolling terrain on this tour should present no problem.

6

Greenville-New Ipswich

28.6 miles; challenging cycling
Hilly terrain

The southern New Hampshire towns of Greenville, Temple, and New Ipswich contrast the ways in which economic growth developed in the state during the nineteenth century. Although they are neighboring towns, each has its own distinctive characteristics.

Greenville was an early mill town that grew up in the 1800s when the agricultural industry began to falter and the manufacture of textiles was introduced to this area along the Souhegan River. The textile industry spread and flourished throughout the state of New Hampshire until the 1930s, when most companies moved to southern states. Many of the abandoned red brick mills lining Greenville's main street had been ignored until recently when restoration was undertaken for current uses as a public library, an inn, and a restaurant, among others.

The other side of nineteenth-century life in the New England of the industrial revolution is represented in the vintage homes of New Ipswich. Its fine white buildings, most notably Barrett House, are authentic and very representative of that era. Near Greenville and New Ipswich lies the tiny hilltop town of Temple, whose Grange Hall testifies to the dominance of agriculture in its past.

These three towns are connected by a network of secondary roads with light traffic and pleasant views. Since there are a number of hills to conquer on the way, this tour is suggested as an all-day trip for those who can accept the challenge of some steep hills to earn the rewards of long downgrades.

Two nice old country inns where you might wish to stay on this tour are the Birchwood Inn (878-3285), located on the village green in Temple, and The Ram in the Thicket, located two blocks off NH 101 in Wilton. With seven and eight rooms respectively, advanced reservations are strongly suggested at both inns especially in July, August, and during foliage season. Dinner at the Birchwood is by reservation only. The Ram in the Thicket serves dinner to guests and the public every night, continental breakfast to guests only, and with some advanced notice, will pack you a box lunch to take with you on your tour. Both places also allow you to park your bike in the barn out of harm's way.

The tour begins at the south end of Greenville at the junction of NH 123 and NH 45. Leave your car along Mill Street (NH 45), which offers ample parking.

0.0   From the junction, proceed north on Mill Street for 0.4 mile, where NH 45 makes a ninety-degree turn to the left up a steep hill.

The red brick mill structures of Greenville and the old railroad station, which has been converted into the Depot Restaurant, provide a vivid picture of nineteenth-century industrial life.

There are several grocery stores in the center of Greenville, and, of course, you can dine in the Depot Restaurant (11:30–2, 5–9 Wed.–Sat.). In addition to the Depot Restaurant, there are several other restaurants in town. You might try the Greenville Inn (878-2761) on the left just a few yards up Mill Street from your starting point. In continuous operation since 1860, this attractive red brick inn is open 11:30–10 daily. In addition, there is a Sunday brunch 9–1.

NH 45 is quite narrow as it climbs out of Greenville. However, it runs through a residential area and the traffic generally travels slowly.

0.4   At the turn, follow the numbered highway 0.7 mile uphill and then another 3.4 miles to the town of Temple.

From the top of the hill on NH 45 north of Greenville center you are

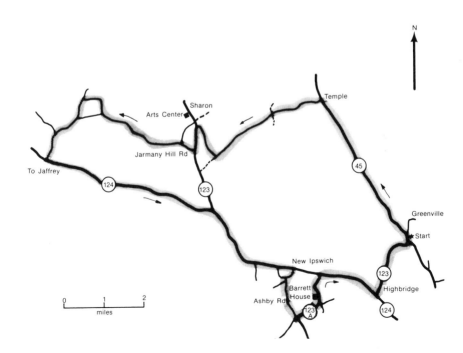

treated to a fine view of the surrounding mountains.

At the top of the hill, NH 45 widens and the pavement is smooth, although the shoulder is bumpy. Traffic is generally light.

4.5   Just before you reach the cluster of buildings in the center of Temple, turn left onto the unsigned road to Sharon. (This road is called West Rd. in Temple, and then changes to Nashua Rd. farther west.) Ride for 3 miles, always staying on the hard surfaced road, to a paved road on the right.

In Temple you can buy food at the general store (7:30–6 Mon.–Sat., 10–1 Sun.) adjacent to the post office.

Birchwood Inn, described in the introduction to this tour, is located on the village green nearby.

From Temple to Sharon the roads are typical of backcountry New Hampshire: narrow, winding, hilly, with overhanging trees, no shoulders, frost heaves, and very little traffic.

7.5   At this intersection, turn right onto the paved road and cycle for 0.4 mile to another junction.

7.9   At this intersection, bear right again and ride 0.6 mile downhill to the junction of NH 123.

Across NH 123 and just to your left is the Sharon Arts Center, which displays and sells works of art and crafts created by New Hampshire artisans. A gallery and shop are open all year (10–5 Mon.–Sat., 1–5 Sun.). Classes are also conducted year-round.

8.5   From the intersection, head south on NH 123 for 0.7 mile to Jarmany Hill Road.

NH 123 is a two-lane road with a smooth surface, no shoulder, and moderate traffic.

9.2   At this intersection turn right and follow Jarmany Hill Road 3.5 miles to a yield sign. Note that after 2.6 miles Spring Hill Road enters from the left. Bear right at this junction and stay on Jarmany Hill Road.

Jarmany Hill Road is a winding, narrow country road. Because traffic is very light, it is ideal for biking.

12.7   At the yield sign, turn left and proceed for 1 mile to a brown house at the foot of a hill, where the road forks. Bear left up a short hill for 0.3 mile on the unsigned hard-packed dirt road (Witt Hill Rd.) and ride another 0.6 mile to NH 124. You will probably need to walk up the hill as the road is steep and rutted, but the remaining section is generally well graded and ridable.

14.6   Turn left onto NH 124, which merges with NH 123 in 4.5 miles, and continue a total of 7 miles to Dark Lane Road, to your right on the outskirts of New Ipswich. Watch for a large building with brown-stained siding on your right at this intersection.

NH 124 is a fairly level, smooth, two-lane road with moderate traffic. For the first mile, its shoulder is gravel, but the roadway then widens with a paved shoulder suitable for cycling. After merging with NH 123, the road climbs for 0.7 mile before leveling off again. Over this uphill stretch the highway is narrow and the paved shoulder disappears, so caution is urged. Beyond the hill, the road again has a decent shoulder.

21.6   Turn right onto Dark Lane Road, riding uphill for 0.5 mile to Ashby Road. Dark Lane Road is a narrow, lightly traveled country lane.

22.1   Turn left onto Ashby Road and follow it downhill for 0.9 mile through pretty surroundings—birch trees, stone walls, and attractive old homes—to NH 123A, also called the Smithville Road.

There's an excellent view of the mountains to the north just as you turn onto Ashby Road. Further along, there is Appleton Manor Farm, a well-landscaped horse farm with a winding gas-lit driveway, white-fenced paddocks, and barns.

23.0   At the intersection with NH 123A, turn left to follow the numbered route 1.5 miles through New Ipswich, where you rejoin NH 123/NH 124.

Take some time to enjoy the fine old buildings lining the road into New Ipswich: the Congregational Church, Town Hall (1817), Friendship Manor, Parsonage, and Barrett House, a Federal-style mansion built

A visit to Barrett House is an appropriate change of pace for the touring cyclist.

shortly after 1800 and furnished with exceptionally fine period pieces. It is open to the public from June to October, Tuesday through Saturday 11–5. There is a small admission charge.

Food is available at Phil's Market (7–9 daily) at the junction of NH 123A and NH 123/NH 124.

1808 House Restaurant, located directly across the street from Phil's Market in a large old colonial, is a family style restaurant open for breakfast, lunch and dinner all day every day except Monday.

NH 123A is a narrow, winding road through a residential area, but that should not present a problem, since most traffic obeys the low speed limit.

24.5 At the intersection with NH 123/NH 124, turn right and ride 1.5 miles to Highbridge, where the two numbered routes split again.

New Ipswich Market, located on the left side of NH 123/NH 124 0.1 mile after turning on this road, is open all day every day.

NH 123/NH 124 is again a smooth-surfaced road with a good shoulder and moderate traffic.

26.0 In Highbridge, turn left onto NH 123 and ride 1.6 miles back to Greenville through rolling countryside along the Souhegan River.

Barry's General Store, located at the junction where NH 123 and NH 124 diverge is open all day every day and has deli grinders, sandwiches and some baked goods.

NH 123 has no shoulder, a fair surface, and little traffic.

27.6 You are back at your starting point in Greenville.

Bicycle Repair Services
Happy Day Cycle, Milford (673-5088).

7

Hancock-Peterborough

**17.4 miles; easy to moderate cycling
Rolling terrain, several hills**

Hancock, named for the man who was president of the Continental Congress, a signer of the Declaration of Independence, and the first post-Revolutionary governor of Massachusetts, does not flaunt its history or its charm. Yet, in its quiet way, the town does convey a vivid sense of the past. Known for its most typical old New England Main Street, it brings together in one place all the scattered pieces of an illusive picture of nineteenth-century life: picket fences, a bandstand on the green, the wood frame school, a meeting house and an inn, and stately old homes. But here the past has been adapted to modern-day life; Hancock does not seem contrived or too perfect.

The 1788 Meeting House, whose bell was forged in Paul Revere's foundry, functions today as it did two hundred years ago. The town's Museum of Antiques reinforces these ties with earlier times. Hancock Historical Society (2–4 Wed.–Sat.) is located at the junction of NH 137 and NH 123.

For wonderful country inn accommodations and food, try the John Hancock Inn (525-3318) on the main street (NH 123) of Hancock. In operation since 1789, innkeepers Glynn and Pat Wells still cater to hungry and tired travelers. The Salzburg Inn and Restaurant (924-3808) is located on Steele Road in Peterborough, 1.2 miles west from the junction of Summer Street and Main Street. Here you have the choice of a new motel unit or a room in the old New England Inn. The Folkway (924-3701), 85 Grove Street, Peterborough offers a continental bed and breakfast, but is best know for its music, food and entertainment.

Off the beaten track some eight miles north of Peterborough, Hancock is easy to reach via US 202 and then NH 123 West. Parking does not present a problem as there is usually space along Main Street (NH 123) or by the white clapboard elementary school, where cars can be left for a few hours.

0.0 From the bandstand on the green, take NH 137 south down a steep hill to Middle Road, on the left shortly after the road levels. There is a sign for Sargent Camp at this junction.

In addition to the points of interest already mentioned, look for the Hancock Toy Shop, also on Main Street, where children's furniture and wooden toys are made. The Village Farm sells apples and cider. Both establishments are located near the junction of NH 137 and NH 123.

Hancock Cash Market, across the street from the John Hancock Inn was established in 1878 and is the last store to buy provisions until Peterborough 7.5 miles away. A small grocery store, it is open all day every day.

NH 137 is narrow with a smooth surface, no shoulder, and light traffic.

0.3   By the sign for Sargent Camp, turn left and follow Middle Road, which runs through a mixture of nicely maintained old farms and homes interspersed with woods, for 7.2 miles to Main Street in Peterborough. Note that 1.2 miles beyond the turnoff for Peterborough Players, the road forks. Stay to the left at this junction. Although not clearly marked, the name of the road changes here to Summer Street.

Approximately 1.5 miles from the junction of Middle Road and NH 137, note the sign and right turn for Sargent Camp, a year-round outdoor education center operated by Boston University. It is open to the public (there is a charge) and offers hiking, fishing, swimming, overnight lodging, and meals. For information or reservations, call 525-3311. At 4.1 miles, a left turn leads to the Peterborough Players summer stock theatre. No matinees are offered, but an evening performance is an excellent way to cap a delightful day's bike tour. Reservations are advised (924-7585).

Like NH 137, Middle Road is narrow and carries little traffic. The road surface is not as smooth as NH 137, however. The terrain here is rolling to hilly, with one gradual climb nearly a mile long and several short descents.

7.5   At the intersection, turn right onto Peterborough's Main Street, head up a short steep hill, and continue for 1.8 miles, past the Peterborough playground, to Windy Row Road, on the right.

Eastern Mountain Sports (EMS) (9–6 Mon.–Sat., noon–6 Sun.), a large outdoor equipment retailer, the The Brookstone Company (9–5 every day), a retail and mail order company specializing in well designed tools and hard to find household items, are both headquartered in Peterborough. Both can be reached by turning left at Main Street instead of right and then left again on US 202. Both are on the right, adjacent to one another, 2.7 miles from Main Street. There is a town park on Grove Street, to the right, with picnic tables and shade trees. The Peterborough Historical Society, also on Grove Street, has collections and displays open to the public every afternoon Monday through Friday during the summer.

Peterborough, a town of nearly 5,000, has a number of food stores and restaurants. The A&P in Peterborough Plaza is open 24 hours a day from Monday to Saturday and 8–5 Sunday. The Hollywood Cafe serves lunch 11:30–2 Mon.–Fri., dinner 5–9 Mon.–Sat., closed Sun.

To get there, go directly across Main Street from its junction with Summer Street. It is located a short distance up the street on the right. The Folkway, 85 Grove Street is open 11:30–11:30 Tues.–Sun. Turn left off Main Street, 0.1 mile west from the junction of Summer and Main, and ride 0.4 mile to this lively cafe restaurant which usually has some form of musical entertainment. For quick and easy eating try the Idlenot Restaurant in Peterborough Plaza near the A&P open all day, every day.

Main Street in Peterborough is wide with a good surface but a rough shoulder. Traffic is moderate to heavy, since you are in a densely populated area. Except for one short, steep grade as you go up Main Street, the terrain is not difficult.

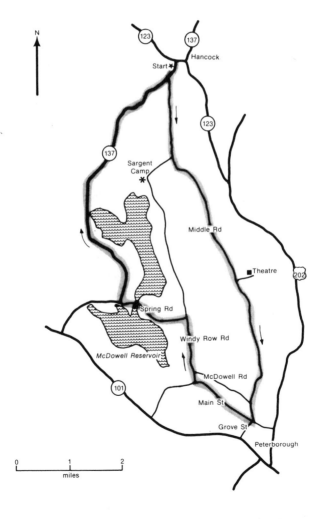

9.3   From Main Street, turn right onto Windy Row Road and begin a gradual
climb past several lovely homes and farms with great views of Pack Monadnock Mountain to the east. In 1.2 miles, just beyond Anandale Farm, you
come to Spring Road, on your left.

The McDowell Colonly, a center for writers, painters, and musicians,
is located on McDowell Road, off Windy Row Road. While not generally open to the public, this retreat has hosted many famous people,
among them Thornton Wilder, who is thought to have written "Our Town"
while in residence here.

Windy Row Road has a fair surface with some frost heaves and
no shoulder. Traffic tends to be light.

10.5   At the junction with Spring Road, turn left and ride 1.3 miles to NH 137.

The Game Preserve on Spring Road is a mini-museum that displays
more than seven hundred early American board and card games.

Spring Road also has a fair surface with some frost heaves and
no shoulder. The way to NH 137 is mostly downhill.

Nicely maintained old farms interspersed with woods characterize much of the
Hancock-Peterborough tour.

11.8   At the junction with NH 137, turn right and follow the numbered route 5.6 miles back to Hancock.

NH 137 is narrow and winding with no shoulder but a good surface. The terrain is rolling and visibility is limited, but traffic is generally light. There is a twisting downgrade for 1.4 miles just before you reach the intersection with Middle Road where you turned off earlier. Because trees along this stretch cast shadows on the roadway, it is often difficult to read the surface accurately. Consequently, caution is advised on this descent.

17.4   You are back at your start by the bandstand in Hancock.

Bicycle Repair Services
Sand Hill Bicycle Shop, Grove St., Peterborough (924-3831).

8

Pierce Homestead-Hillsboro Center

19.8 miles; moderate cycling
Rolling to hilly terrain, several hills

Lovewell Mountain, the fourth highest peak in southern New Hampshire, provides a graceful backdrop for this Currier and Ives tour. But perhaps the most enticing aspect of the trip is the absence of commercial tourism. You can wind unhurriedly along lightly traveled byways and become enveloped by the constantly changing landscape around you — dairy farms with open pasture, thick forests, restored homes set in rural quietude, and small villages with long histories. While recommended as an all-day tour for flower-pickers and picnic-lovers, this trip can be completed in a half-day spurt by those bent on improving their cardio-vascular systems.

There are several places nearby where you can enjoy pleasant accommodations. Fred and Judy Heyliger operate the small, peaceful and intimate Uplands Inn in Antrim Center (588-6349). Full breakfast is included with your stay. The Stonebridge Inn (464-3155), located on NH 9, 1.3 miles east of the junction of NH 9 and NH 31, is a new, little-old country inn with four recently decorated guestrooms. Lunch and dinner are served daily except Monday. Victoria Prewitt's Stonewall Farm Bed and Breakfast (478-5205), located on Black Pond Road in Windsor, 1.1 miles from William's Store, provides another very pleasant overnight stay. The Eighteen Thirty House Motel (478-3155) and Brookwood Motel (478-5258) are both located at the junction of NH 9 and NH 31.

The recommended starting point is the Franklin Pierce Homestead near the intersection of NH 9 and NH 31, three miles west of Hillsboro. A polite request for permission to park generally results in an affirmative reply from the manager.

0.0   From the Franklin Pierce Homestead, travel north on NH 31 for 1.9 miles to a fork in the road. Just before the fork there is a dark brown house with attached barn and a signpost for East Washington on the right.

The Franklin Pierce Homestead is the family home of the fourteenth president of the United States. The house, which is tastefully decorated and furnished with period antiques, is open 10–5 Friday, Saturday, Sunday and holidays from Memorial Day to Labor Day. A small admission fee is charged. Tatewell Gallery (478-5755), selling antiques and collectibles, is located adjacent to the Pierce Homestead.

Manahan Park, operated by the Town of Hillsboro, is located 0.5 mile west on NH 9. It offers a beach and swimming on Pierce Lake.

The Corner Store (7–10 daily) is at the intersection of NH 9 and NH 31. In addition to groceries, it has a very small deli and a counter where you can buy hamburgers and sandwiches. Diamond Acres, located on NH 9 across the street from Manahan Park, is a popular drive-in and snackbar open daily during the summer. William's General Store, 1 mile north on NH 31 is open daily, with shorter hours on Sundays (8–1). This is the last store until Hillsboro, sixteen miles away.

Just a few yards beyond William's Store on the left is Black Pond Road. If you turn left and ride 1.1 miles, you will come to Stonewall Farm Bed and Breakfast.

NH 31, with the exception of the first mile which has recently been reconstructed, is rolling, narrow, and has no shoulder. The road surface is old and rough but quite ridable. Traffic is generally light.

1.9   At the fork, turn right toward East Washington and continue for 3.3 miles
to a T-junction. This section of road is known as Coolidge Road on town
maps, but it is more commonly referred to as the East Washington Road.
Country auctions are held frequently at Crane's Auction Barn 1.8 miles from
the junction of NH 31 and Coolidge Road.

At Lachut's Farm you can watch prize Holsteins grazing. Several antique shops along the way welcome browsers.

Coolidge Road is narrow but generally has a fair surface. The terrain is rolling for about 2 miles followed by one long downgrade.

5.2   At the T-junction, turn left and ride 2 miles through a scenic valley to the
village of East Washington.

The village of East Washington, with towering Lovewell Mountain mir-
rored in its calm pond, impresses the traveler with its quiet serenity.

The two-mile stretch through the valley has no shoulder and many
frost heaves, but, on the positive side, very little traffic.

7.2   From the pond in East Washington, retrace your route for 2 miles to the
T-junction. Proceed straight for 4 miles to Hillsboro Center.

Bear Track Farm Antiques is located on the right side 2.1 miles from
the junction of Coolidge Road and the road to Hillsboro Center.

Hillsboro Center is a small, picturesque community and historic
district. Among its early churches and houses stands the 1773
homestead of its first minister. Although these buildings are not open
to the public, their antiquity makes them of interest to the passerby.

This is a narrow country road with a cracked and bumpy surface.
Again, very light traffic provides freedom for the cyclist. After 1.8 miles
the road begins a gradual rise that continues for 2.2 miles to Hillsboro
Center. The last 0.3 mile is very steep.

13.2   From Hillsboro Center, continue on the same road for 3.6 miles more to
the junction of NH 9 in the town of Hillsboro.

Fox State Forest, a game refuge and forestry research center, is laced
with a network of hiking trails. The open farmland below Hillsboro Center
offers some spectacular views of the mountains of southern New
Hampshire.

Maplewood Farm Antiques is located on the left 4.7 miles from
the junction of Coolidge Road and the Hillsboro Center Road. Open
10–5 daily from May 1 to October 1 and 10–4 Thursday through Sunday from November 1 to April 30.

This stretch of road is somewhat wider and smoother than the previ-
ous one, although it should still be considered very much secondary.
This is all downgrade, the longest coast of the day. Traffic is light.

16.7   In Hillsboro, turn right and ride 1.7 miles on NH 9 to a paved road by a
brick power station at the base of a long hill. Both the power station and
paved road are on the left.

Since Hillsboro is the commercial center of the surrounding towns, a number of stores and restaurants provide food and drink.

NH 9 is a major east-west route and consequently is the only section of the tour that does not provide pleasant cycling. While the speed limit is low, traffic can be moderate to heavy, and the shoulder is inadequate for cycling.

18.4   By the power station, turn left onto the unmarked paved road (Saw Hill Road) and follow it for 1.4 miles to the intersection of NH 9 and NH 31.

Saw Hill Road is a return to narrow, bumpy road conditions with very little traffic.

Many of the uncongested country roads in the Hillsboro area are ideal for family biking.

19.8   You are back at the Franklin Pierce Homestead at the junction of NH 9 and
NH 31.

Bicycle Repair Services
Ped'ling Fool, 77 West Main St., Hillsboro (464-5286). Hours: 10–1 Mon., Tues.,
    Thurs., Fri.; 9–5 Sat.

9

Crotched Mountain-Colby Hill

The distance, difficulty, and terrain are stated at the beginning of each day's directions.

Bicycling is an activity easily adapted to personal tastes, desires, and attitudes. With possibilities ranging from an evening ride around the block to an extended cross-country tour, only the imagination limits how the simple, efficient, nonpolluting bicycle can be used as a source of recreation and adventure. For variety, try coupling an active day of cycling with an overnight stay in the warm, inviting atmosphere of an old New England inn. They are found in the various nooks and crannies of New Hampshire, and each has a character all its own molded by the personalities of many generations of innkeepers and the weathering of New England seasons. You should expect the floors to slant and the stairs to creak, for these are signs of respectability and endearment, a form of homage to an elder statesman. And after a day of riding, a hot bath, a home-cooked dinner, and a warm bed, you feel like you have come to visit with an old friend in the country.

This tour offers a few inns conveying such warmth and friendliness: The Crotched Mountain Inn in Francestown, the Colby Hill Inn in Henniker and the Meeting House Inn and Restaurant (428-3536), also located in Henniker at the base of Pat's Peak Ski Area. Conveniently accessible to each other by bicycle, they are joined by a network of roads through small towns and appealing countryside. We have designed this trip for the weekend cyclist who seeks to combine a healthy dose of moderate exercise with the warm atmosphere of a friendly home.

We suggest you start at the Crotched Mountain Inn, located adjacent to Crotched Mountain Ski Area, off NH 47, 3.6 miles north of Francestown. The Inn is an old rambling brick and wood colonial. With a spectacular view of southern New Hampshire from the lawn, it sets the perfect tone for your two-day trip. Call ahead for reservations (588-6840 or 588-6841), and then plan to arrive in the afternoon or early evening in time to enjoy the tennis courts and pool. The innkeepers, John and Rose Perry, go out of their way to provide you with an enjoyable stay.

The Colby Hill Inn, located on Western Avenue 0.5 mile west of its junction with NH 114 in Henniker, is a lovely colonial house built around 1800. The congenial members of the Glover family are both the proprietors and hosts at the inn. They offer elegant yet comfortable accommodations and dining for their guests and the public (dinner is served every day but Monday). For reservations for your overnight stay call 428-3281.

Day One
21.4 miles; moderate cycling
Rolling terrain

0.0   Begin your tour from the Crotched Mountain Inn by riding 1 mile back to NH 47.

1.0   When you reach NH 47, turn left and ride for 4.6 miles to Bennington.
            A number of antique shops along this route invite browsing. In this part of southern New Hampshire you ride through picture-postcard villages and countryside.
            NH 47 is a narrow, winding road with a smooth surface, light traffic, and no shoulder. Because you are heading away from Crotched Mountain, the land generally slopes downward, making cycling easy.
            At the junction of NH 31 and NH 47 in Bennington, turn right and ride 0.1 mile to a fork in the road. Bear left and ride along the Contoocook River, past the Monadnock Paper Mill to the junction of US 202.
            If you have time to explore, turn left at the junction of NH 47 and NH 31, and ride 0.1 mile on NH 31 to get to Bennington Country Store (open all day, every day). It offers food and beverages for the weary.
            Back on the tour just after you take the left fork off of NH 31 and NH 47, you will come to Alberto's Restaurant serving Italian food from 5 PM daily except Sunday.

6.3   At the junction, turn right onto US 202/NH 31 and ride for 1.7 miles through Antrim, where the numbered highways split.
            Roger's Country Store and Wayno's, both located in downtown Antrim are open all day, everyday.
            US 202, a major route, has a smooth surface, an intermittent shoulder, good visibility, and generally light to moderate traffic.

8.0   When the numbered highways divide, bear right on US 202 and ride 6 miles to Hillsboro, where US 202 joins NH 9.
            About 1.5 miles beyond Antrim you reach a section of US 202 with a wide paved shoulder, which continues for 3.3 miles.

14.0   At the junction in Hillsboro, turn right onto US 202/NH 9 and ride for 3 miles through town to River Road, on the right.
            There are numerous grocery stores and restaurants located in Hillsboro. The Stonebridge Inn, a lovely old colonial structure located 0.3 mile west from the junction of NH 9 and US 202, serves lunch and dinner daily except Monday (464-3155).
            The section of US 202/NH 9 through Hillsboro has no shoulder and moderate to heavy traffic, especially on weekends. However, the

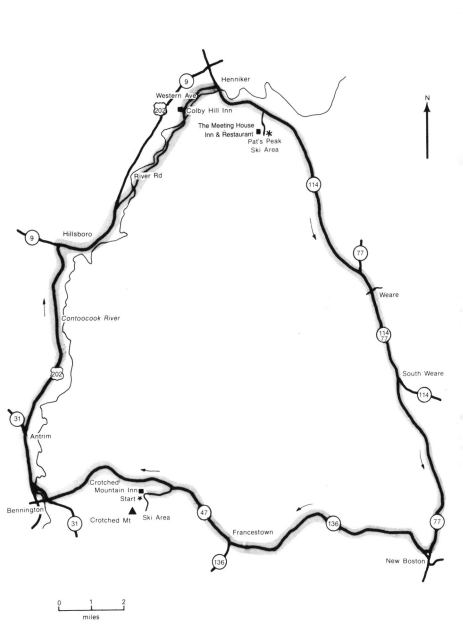

speed limit is low and the visibility is good. Just as you reach what is obviously new pavement, you come to your turn by River Road.

17.0   At the intersection of River Road, by the sign for West Henniker, turn right and cycle for 4.4 miles to Colby Hill Inn, on your left. River Road is the old Route 202. It is called River Road as you turn on to it just east of Hillsboro. There is a sign post. River Road crosses the Contoocook 1.5 miles west of NH 114. The name changes from River Road to Western Ave. when it crosses the river. It hugs the south bank of the Contoocook and there is no chance of getting lost.

River Road has a smooth surface, no shoulder, many curves, and several short, steep hills. Because it parallels the Contoocook River downstream, the riding is generally easy.

21.4   You are at Colby Hill Inn, your destination on Day One of this tour.

Day Two
28.2 miles; moderate cycling
Rolling terrain

0.0   From Colby Hill Inn, continue along River Road, now called Western Avenue, 0.6 mile to the center of Henniker.

Henniker is home to New England College, a small, liberal arts school with approximately one thousand students. There is plenty of winter recreation at Pat's Peak, a popular regional ski area, and when the snow melts, outdoor enthusiasts head for The Biking Expedition, Inc., a student bicycle travel program which offers trips in the US, Canada and Europe.

For food and beverages, there are three stores in downtown Henniker: Baldwins Market (8–6 Mon.–Sat., closed Sun.), Preston Block Market (open all day, every day), and Pop Schultz's Market (open all day, every day) which makes great sandwiches.

In addition to fine food at the Colby Hill Inn or The Meeting House, several other restaurants in Henniker have excellent cusine. Daniel's Pub (11:30–10:30 Mon.–Sat., 5–10 Sun., 428-7621), downtown near Baldwin's Market, offers homemade soups, sandwiches, daily specials, and full course dinners in a pleasant setting overlooking the Contoocook River. Country Spirit Restaurant (11–3, 5–9 Mon.–Sat., 11–9 Sun., 428-7007), at the junction of NH 9 and NH 114, offers daily specials, full course dinners, and a bar/lounge.

0.6   In Henniker, turn right onto NH 114 and continue for 11.1 miles to the junction of NH 114 and NH 77 in South Weare.

Between Henniker and South Weare there are a number of stores where you can purchase sandwiches and snacks including Country Maid Market at 1.6 miles, Crosby's Store at 7.3 miles, Weare Central Store and Gift Shop at 9 miles, and Country 3 Corners at 11.7 miles. With the exception of Weare Central Store, which is closed Monday, all are open all day every day. Weare Subs and Pizza at 8.4 miles is also open all day Mon.–Sat. and 11–8 on Sunday.

NH 114 is rolling to hilly, with downgrades in your favor. The shoulder varies from one that is wide and paved, suitable for biking, to nothing at all. Visibility is generally very good except for the 2-mile stretch just before the center of Weare. There, the road curves over hilly terrain, and we urge caution. While traffic is normally light to moderate, some large trucks do use this route.

11.7 In South Weare, turn right onto NH 77 toward New Boston. In 5.8 miles, just as you come into the village, you intersect NH 136.

In New Boston you can purchase food at Dodge's General Store (Est. 1872). From the junction of NH 77 and NH 136 continue south for 0.3 mile to the junction of NH 13. Turn left and ride 0.1 mile to Dodge's.

This group of tourers prepares to start out from the Colby Hill Inn in Henniker, one of New Hampshire's many fine country inns.

The Molly Stark Tavern, located on NH 13, 0.5 mile south of the junction of NH 77 and NH 136, is an excellent restaurant serving traditional cuisine (Lunch, 11:30–2 Wed.–Fri.; Dinner 5–9:30 Wed.–Sat. and 1–8 Sun., closed Mon. and Tues.; for reservations call 487-2733).

NH 77 has a good surface but very little shoulder. Normally traffic is light. The terrain is rolling, generally in your favor.

17.5 At the junction in New Boston, turn right onto NH 136 and ride for 6.9 miles to Francestown.

One-half mile before the center of Francestown you pass a historical marker describing a nearby quarry that once yielded high-quality soapstone.

The Vadney General Store (7–6 Mon.–Sat., closed for lunch noon–1; 9–12 Sun.), is located on NH 47 in the center of Francestown.

When you turn onto NH 136, you begin a gradual climb that continues all the way back to the Crotched Mountain Inn. It should not present a problem to most cyclists, however. This route is rather curvy with no shoulder and very little traffic.

24.4 In Francestown, turn right onto NH 47 and cycle 2.8 miles back to the road to the Crotched Mountain Ski Area and the inn.

27.2 At the junction of NH 47 and Mountain Road, turn left to cycle the last mile of your tour.

Grandmother's House, a fine restaurant located at the junction of NH 47 and Mountain Road, serves American and European food (closed Monday; for reservations, call 588-2355.)

28.2 You are back at the Crotched Mountain Inn, where you began your two-day tour.

Bicycle Repair Services
Ped'ling Fool, 77 West Main St., Hillsboro (464-5286). Hours: 10–1 Mon., Tues., Thurs., Fri.: 9–5 Sat.

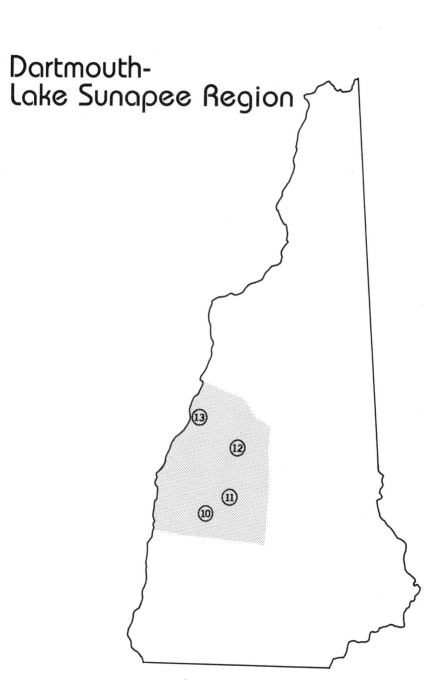

Dartmouth-
Lake Sunapee Region

10

Lake Sunapee Loop

23.2 miles; challenging cycling
Rolling to very hilly terrain

With its pine-covered islands, twenty-nine miles of jagged coastline, and crystal water, Lake Sunapee epitomizes the beauty of this rugged part of the Granite State. Mount Sunapee, third highest peak in southern New Hampshire, rises steeply from its western shore and provides a precipitous backdrop to this popular summer resort area. Because it is a retreat for those who enjoy fishing, swimming, and boating, our trip around the lake is highly recommended for early fall or late spring, the between-season times when snow-lovers and water-lovers are shifting gears.

And speaking of gears, this trip offers an excellent opportunity to refine your gear-shifting technique and to test your hill climbing philosophy. With a number of long, steep grades to conquer, both mind and body face a challenge. It also provides an opportunity to pit your cycling ability against that of others, for this is the route of the popular Sunapee Bike Race, held annually during the last weekend in August. If you wish to try your luck, you can enter the citizen's race. The large number of participants are divided into categories based on age: Juniors (eighteen years and under), Seniors (nineteen to twenty-nine), and Veterans (over thirty). Serious racers enter the U.S. Cycling Federation portion of the race and must circle the twenty-two mile course four times. Should the prospect of such intense competition turn you off, take the trip on a cool, mid-September day when you can ride the loop at your own leisurely pace.

Because it is a popular resort area, the Lake Sunapee Region has numerous establishments offering dining and lodging. For a map and listing of these places as well as the area's attractions and recreational facilities, write the Lake Sunapee Business Association, Box 400, Sunapee, NH 03782 or call toll free from outside of New Hampshire at 800-258-3530.

The Bed and Breakfast in Georges Mills (763-9782) on NH 11 is a pleasant and convenient place to spend the night. Breakfast is also served to the public 7–noon, Monday through Saturday (closed Tuesday) and 9–1 Sunday. Loma Lodge Bed and Breakfast (763-4849) on NH 103B, 1.2 miles from the Sunapee traffic circle is another good choice. Located in a recently restored 200-year-old colonial, the lodge has private rooms as well as a bunk room for the budget conscious.

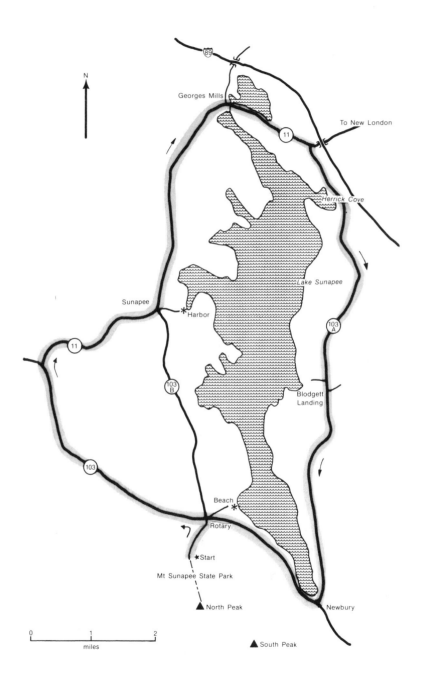

The nearest bicycle shops are located in New London. See the New London Lakes tours for details.

Begin your trip at the ski area parking lot in Mount Sunapee State Park, located off NH 103 in Newbury. Simply follow the signs to the rotary by the park entrance and take the access road 0.7 mile uphill to its end by the base lodge.

0.0 From the parking lot, coast .7 mile back to NH 103, turn left, and head north on NH 103 for 4 miles to NH 11.

Mount Sunapee State Park offers a bit of something for everyone. For a nominal admission, you can swim at the park's sandy beach on Lake Sunapee, which can be reached from the well-marked access road off the rotary. A changing house is available, and a life guard is on duty during the summer months. Picnicking facilities, hiking trails, and a gondola to the top of Mount Sunapee are all located adjacent to the parking lot at the base of the ski slopes. During the first week in August the League of New Hampshire Craftsmen holds its annual fair here, and while this is a worthwhile event to attend, the unusually high volume of traffic that it generates causes hazardous cycling conditions. Consequently, extreme caution is advised if you plan to cycle this route then.

A snack bar is located in both the base and summit lodges at the park. Perkins General Store (7:30–5 daily) is situated on the right just north of the Mount Sunapee rotary on NH 103.

NH 103 is a wide, two-lane road over rolling terrain with a smooth surface and paved shoulder suitable for biking. It offers excellent visibility and generally light to moderate traffic; during peak summer weekend hours the highway can be very busy, however.

4.7 At the junction of NH 103 and NH 11, turn right onto NH 11 and ride for 7.6 miles to NH 103A, just before the I-89 underpass. Note the sign for Newbury and Blodgett Landing.

Sunapee Harbor just off the main route makes a pleasant rest stop. Turn right at the blinking yellow light on NH 11, 2.5 miles beyond NH 103, and ride 0.5 mile to the water's edge. Should you wish an even closer look at the lake, the *M.V. Mount Sunapee* offers cruises daily 10:30 AM and 2:30 PM from June 27 to Labor Day (763-5430). The *Sunapee Belle* offers a dockside lunch noon–1:30 and dining cruises on the lake at 5:45 and 7:45, also from June 27 to Labor Day (763-5477).

Several grocery stores, snack bars, and restaurants are located around Sunapee Harbor. Sunapee Community Store and Barton's Mart, located at Sunapee Harbor 0.2 and 0.4 mile respectively from NH 11, are both open all day, every day. The Dockside Restaurant, overlooking the harbor, and Woodbine Cottages, located across from the marina are two good places to eat. The Dockside is good for sandwiches and snacks while Woodbine Cottages, serving breakfast, lunch, and dinner, specializes in more elegant dining. Gardeners General Store (open all day, every day), on NH 11 in Georges Mills 0.5 mile before the junction with NH 103A, is the last place to buy food until you reach Newbury.

Like NH 103, NH 11 is a wide two-lane highway with a smooth surface, paved shoulder, and light to moderate traffic conditions along much of the way. The terrain however is much more hilly, and there is one long steep hill just beyond the turn to Sunapee Harbor. Two miles beyond the same turn, the shoulders become intermittent and often unridable.

12.3   Following the sign to Blodgett Landing and Newbury, turn right and proceed south on NH 103A for 7.9 miles to its junction with NH 103 in Newbury.

Watch for the historical marker 0.8 mile south on NH 103A. During the golden age of steamboating on Lake Sunapee, the *Kearsarge, Ascutney, Armenia White,* and others brought hundreds of passengers to this location on Herrick Cove. From here they were transported by stage to New London's hotels and boarding houses. A lovely stone barn is situated on the right 6.2 miles from the junction of NH 11.

Frostop Snackbar, the Newbury Harbor Restaurant and Pub and the Lake Sunapee Trading Post General Store are all clustered together on NH 103 just after you turn off NH 103A onto NH 103. All are open daily during summer months.

Spring, summer, and fall, the Lake Sunapee area attracts cyclists who seek ideal biking roads.

NH 103A is narrow, with no shoulder but a smooth surface. While it carries less traffic than NH 103 and NH 11, it does have the steepest hills on the trip. However, because of the hills, the countryside is scenic and numerous old summer homes complement the landscape.

20.2 At the junction in Newbury, turn right and ride 2.3 miles to the Mount Sunapee rotary.

NH 103 from Newbury to the rotary is rolling and wide with a smooth surface and a paved shoulder.

22.5 At the rotary, turn left and climb 0.7 mile back uphill to the parking lot and your car.

23.2 Your tour ends here at the base of Mount Sunapee.

11

New London Lakes: Two short tours

**The distance, difficulty, and terrain are stated at the beginning
of each trip's directions.**

It is little wonder that New London has long been a focal point of recreational activity in the Dartmouth–Lake Sunapee Region, for this hilltop town is surrounded by lakes and commands an exceptional view of 2,937-foot Mount Kearsarge. Situated at the northern end of Lake Sunapee, its history as a resort dates back to earlier times, before the internal combustion engine, when trains, steamboats, and carriages would deliver summer vacationers from Boston to its inns and hotels. Its Main Street still has ties to the past with fine old colonials, several inviting inns, and the red brick and mortar buildings of Colby-Sawyer College. Today New London functions both as a residential community and a year-round recreational center. Within easy reach of three major ski areas, three state parks, and numerous lakes, it is an ideal place for a holiday.

New London also offers interesting possibilities for cyclists. We have chosen here to describe two short, half-day trips, so those who might wish to couple cycling with other activities can do so easily. Because they are short, they are particularly suitable for those new to cycle touring, and while New London's location on a hilltop means negotiating several steep hills on the final leg of both tours, the climbs should cause no traumatic aftereffects. Those wanting a longer day of riding can easily combine the two trips in a figure-eight pattern or take the Lake Sunapee trip described previously (see tour 10). Perhaps the most enticing way to approach your holiday here is to combine cycling with an overnight stay at one of several quality inns in the area. The New London Inn (526-2791), located adjacent to Colby-Sawyer College on Main Street in New London is a gracious old house that dates to 1792. Hide-away Lodge (526-4861), near Little Lake Sunapee offers eight guest rooms in an intimate house with a kitchen that is well-known for exceptional food prepared by innkeeper Wolf Heinberg. Pleasant Lake Inn (526-6271) which you pass on the Pleasant Lake loop, was converted from a farm to an inn over 100 years ago. Finally, Maple Hill Farm (526-2248), a Bed and Breakfast on the Newport Road/Otterville Road Junction, is a comfortable 1825 New England farm recently renovated for its present use.

Both tours begin in the center of New London at the parking lot across the street from New London Trust.

Little Lake Sunapee
10.5 miles; moderate cycling
Hilly terrain

0.0   From the parking lot, turn left onto Main Street and proceed for 0.5 mile, passing both the Edgewood Inn (no lodging offered) and the New London Barn Players Theater, to the blinking yellow light, where the road forks.

New London's Main Street has a variety of shops and well-kept old buildings. There are several food stores in New London. Diagonally across from the parking lot where you start your trip is Jiffy Mart, open all day every day. Cricenti's is a large supermarket located on the Newport Road 1.1 miles northwest of your starting point.

For those who prefer restaurants, try Peter Christian's Tavern (11:30–12:30), in the Edgewood Inn a few blocks north on Main Street, which specializes in hearty soups, salads, sandwiches, and quiches. The Millstone on Newport Road is another casually elegant restaurant open 11:30–2:30 for lunch and from 5:30 for dinner.

Main Street is wide and level with moderate traffic and good visibility.

0.5   At the junction, continue straight on the right fork to Little Sunapee Lake. The road toward Little Sunapee Lake offers views of the surrounding countryside before it actually descends to the lakeshore. Bucklin Beach, which you reach about 1 mile from the fork, offers fine swimming during the summer.

The route to Little Sunapee Lake is a narrow, twisting, two-lane road with a smooth surface and generally light traffic over hilly terrain.

2.1   At the sharp curve just beyond Bucklin Beach, bear left along the lakeshore, following the signs to Springfield and Grantham.

3.8   When the road begins to ascend gradually while curving right, another sign for Springfield and Grantham comes into view. Here, turn left onto a small unmarked road and ride for 1.6 miles to Otterville Road.

From the junction with the unmarked road to NH 11, which Otterville Road intersects, you travel narrow, hilly backcountry roads with some frost heaves and limited visibility.

5.4   At Otterville Road, turn right and ride for 1.1 miles to NH 11.

Otter Pond near the junction of Otterville Road and NH 11 offers fine swimming from the picnic area.

6.5   At the intersection, turn left onto NH 11 and ride for 0.8 mile to the I-89 and NH 11 interchange and then 3.2 miles on Main Street back to the center of New London.

NH 11 is a two-lane road with a smooth surface, wide, paved shoulders, excellent visibility, and moderate traffic.

10.5   You are back at the start of this short trip.

Pleasant Lake
14.9 miles; moderate to challenging cycling
Hilly terrain

0.0   From the parking lot opposite the New London Trust, turn right onto Main Street and cycle for 1.6 miles past the New London Inn and Colby-Sawyer College, both on your left, to the traffic light where Main Street intersects NH 11.

Colby-Sawyer College, founded in 1837, enrolls around seven hundred women and offers degree programs in liberal arts and medical technology. As you coast down to the intersection of Main Street and NH 11 a panoramic view of Mount Kearsarge and adjacent mountains unfolds, a prelude to what you see on the fantastic downgrade on the next stretch to Wilmot Flat.

In addition to stores and restaurants already mentioned, you pass on this tour the Grey House (11:30–9 daily). At the junction of Main Street and NH 11, it offers everything from ice cream cones to a full-course dinner.

Main Street is wide with good visibility, moderate traffic, and an intermittent shoulder. Exercise caution on the steep downgrade just before the junction.

1.6   At the intersection, turn left onto NH 11 and ride downhill for 3.7 miles to the turnoff for Wilmot Flat.

The views of Kearsarge and surrounding mountains on this stretch are breath-taking.

NH 11 along this downhill section is a wide, two-lane road with good visibility and an excellent paved shoulder suitable for cycling.

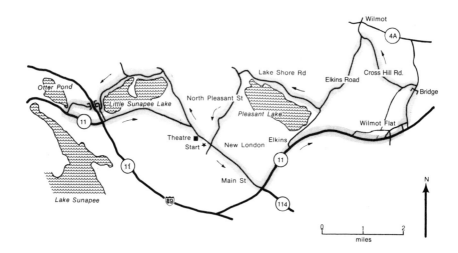

5.3   At the turnoff, turn left and ride for 0.1 mile to a T-junction in Wilmot Flat. The roads from Wilmot Flat back to New London are generally narrow, curvy, and hilly with poor visibility but very low traffic. They vary from a relatively smooth surface to bumpy with a fair number of frost heaves.

5.4   At the T-junction in Wilmot Flat, turn right and ride past the post office to another T-junction.

5.5   At this junction, turn left onto the road to Wilmot and proceed for 1 mile to a road on the left just beyond a narrow bridge.

6.5   Just beyond the narrow bridge, turn left onto Cross Hill Road (unmarked) and ride 0.2 mile to a fork. Take the right fork and continue up a long gradual hill for 1.8 miles to a crossroad and a sign for New London pointing left.

8.5   At the crossroad, turn left onto Elkins Road (unmarked) heading for New London and ride 2 miles to a fork in the road.

Part of the fun of touring in New Hampshire is encountering the unexpected – in this case a huge yard sale.

10.5   At this junction, bear right onto Lake Shore Road and continue for 2.7 miles. The road will bear to the left as it becomes North Pleasant Road. Follow this road another 1.7 miles back to your starting point.

From the Pleasant Lake Inn, you are treated to a great view of the lake. A historical marker near the inn recalls the exploits of the Pleasant Street Pioneers.

If you continue straight instead of turning right onto Lake Shore Road, you come in 0.3 mile to a small store in Elkins.

14.9   Your tour ends on Main Street in the center of New London.

Bicycle Repair Services

Crossroads Sport Shop, Main St., New London (526-4071).
Kiernan's Bicycle Shop, Main St., New London (526-4948).

12

Canaan-Newfound Lake

54.5 miles; challenging cycling
Rolling to hilly terrain

Here is a trip for those who are primarily interested in a full day of rugged cycling. Bounded by the towns of Plymouth, Franklin, and Enfield, the rural area this tour circles through has until recently been forgotten by the tourists and developers attracted to the more glamorous Seacoast, Lakes, and White Mountain regions. It was perhaps the best-kept secret around, but people are now beginning to discover its clear lakes, rushing streams, and formidable mountains. While growth extending east from Hanover and west from Plymouth and Franklin may change the face of this part of New Hampshire in years to come, it is, for the immediate future at least, an excellent place to enjoy long distance rural cycling. Suggested for the more experienced cyclist, the ride offers long stretches where you can find a quiet unity of man and machine and relish the pace and rhythm of uninterrupted movement. With the exception of the stretch along the western shore of Newfound Lake, you should encounter little traffic. Unlike most of our other tours, this one does not offer numerous historic or architectural points of interest. Its beauty is to be found in waterfalls, sculptured rocks, and the other natural phenomena in which man has played little part.

Several inns and Bed and Breakfast establishments are located on or near the route you travel. The Grafton Inn (523-4591) on US 4 in Grafton (adjacent to the Grafton General Store) is built in the Victorian style. It offers home cooking and is a favorite watering hole for passing cyclists who fill their water bottles from the inn's Artesian well. If you can't stay at the inn, you can use the shower facilities for $2.50. Six Chimneys Bed and Breakfast (744-2029) on NH 3A in East Hebron is a lovely 1790 colonial, once used as an eighteenth century coach stop. The owners, Mr. and Mrs. Peter Fortescue, lived in both England and Spain and have decorated the house with antiques from both countries. A large and tasty breakfast is another highlight for cyclists who stay here. The Inn at Danbury (768-3318) on NH 104, 0.5 mile from Danbury Center is particularly suited to the cyclist because in addition to the inn, there is also a bicycle shop open from mid-May through September. It also houses the New England Bicycling Center, a program designed to teach young, aspiring cyclists the skills and techniques of bicycle racing.

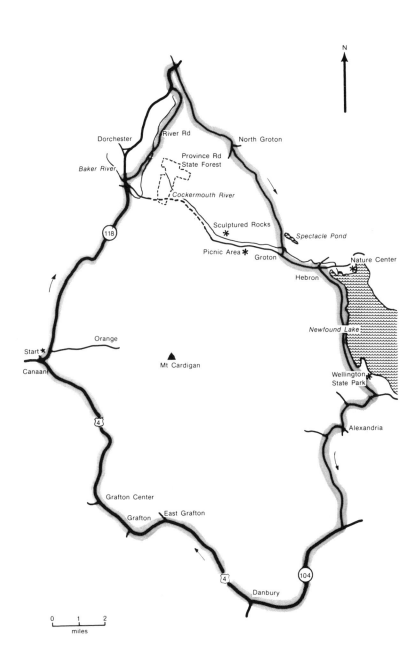

N

Dorchester

River Rd

North Groton

Province Rd
State Forest

Baker River

Cockermouth River

118

Sculptured Rocks

Spectacle Pond

Picnic Area *

Groton

Nature Center

Hebron

Newfound Lake

Orange

Start *

Mt Cardigan

Canaan

Wellington
State Park

4

Alexandria

Grafton Center

Grafton   East Grafton

4

104

Danbury

0   1   2
miles

Begin the trip in Canaan at the junction of US 4 and NH 118 near the east end of the main street. Parking should present no problem.

0.0   From the junction in Canaan, head north on NH 118 for 8 miles to paved River Road, on the right. This road is approximately 0.2 mile beyond the dirt crossroad that leads on the right to Province Road State Forest. If you find yourself in the tiny village of Dorchester, you have continued too far on NH 118.

You come to the turnoff for Cardigan State Park approximately 0.5 mile north of Canaan on NH 118. While the park offers both picnicking and good hiking trails, we don't recommend that you make the detour unless you have plenty of time and energy. It is a 4-mile ride, sometimes uphill, into the park and another 4 miles back out, which would add considerably to an already long day. If you're bounding with energy, you may wish a shorter side trip to Cilley's Cave, where a hermit lived for nearly forty years. To get there, take the road to Cardigan State Park only as far as the town hall in Orange, park your bike, and then hike up the Orange Pond Trail, which starts behind the town hall.

The Canaan Country Store (523-7578), Jesse's Market (523-4833) both on US 4, and Canaan Cash Market (523-4362) on Depot Street are three places to purchase food in Canaan. All three are open all day, seven days a week.

NH 118 is a two-lane road with an adequate biking surface and an unridable gravel shoulder. It is fairly level as you leave Canaan, but you will encounter some hills as you go farther north.

8.0   At River Road, turn right and proceed alongside the Baker River for 4.4 miles until you rejoin NH 118.

As you enjoy the pleasant downgrade along the Baker River's east side, keep an eye out for waterfalls and cascades.

River Road, although paved, is narrow and has a rough surface, but virtually no traffic. You should not have trouble cycling.

12.4   When you reach NH 118, turn right and ride for 1 mile to a four-way junction at the foot of a hill (approximately 0.5 mile beyond the Dorchester General Store).

The Dorchester General Store (6–7:30 daily, closed Mon., 786-9222) offers a snack bar, supplies, home-baked muffins, and outstanding hospitality. It is your last opportunity to buy food until you reach Hebron, eleven miles further on.

This stretch of NH 118 is similar to the one you were on earlier.

13.4   At the junction in the town of Cheever, turn sharply right to head towards Groton. The sign for Groton, on the right, is easy to miss, so watch carefully.

This road is a narrow, country byway with no shoulder, very little traffic, and, generally, a rough surface. Over the first 1.9 miles you climb, sometimes steeply; then for the next 1.8 miles you descend through pleasant, open countryside.

17.1   At the bottom of the hill in North Groton, at the fork, follow the main road as it heads to the right over a short bridge. There are signs here for Wellington State Park and Bristol, both of which are well beyond your next turn, which is 4.8 miles away in Groton.

The road continues as a narrow byway with a generally rough surface. You climb again for 0.9 mile but are rewarded with a fantastic and often steep descent 3 miles long. The last 0.9 mile to Groton is fairly level.

The rivers and streams in the secluded region north of Canaan have carved potholes and wading pools.

21.9   At the intersection in Groton, turn sharply left to stay on the main road. Note another sign for Wellington State Park and Bristol pointing in your direction of travel. For 1.7 miles you ride through reasonably level valley farmland to the town of Hebron.

If you turn right at the intersection in Groton onto the minor road and ride 1.1 miles, you will come to Sculptured Rocks Geologic Site, part of the New Hampshire Division of Parks. Glaciers have sculptured potholes and rocks in the Cockermouth River that make great sliding and swimming platforms. There are also walking trails along the river and plenty of places to picnic.

23.6   At the village green in Hebron, turn right onto West Shore Road, which you follow 5.6 miles along Newfound Lake to a stop sign.

Hebron is a pretty New Hampshire town with a schoolhouse, church, and general store fronting a gas-lit green. If instead of turning right you continue straight for approximately 1 mile, through Hebron, staying to the right of the green, you come to Paradise Point Audubon Nature Center at the northern end of Newfound Lake. It features natural history, environmental and wildlife exhibits, nature walks, and films. The Center is open daily from the last week in June through Labor Day 10–5. A donation of $1 for adults and $.50 for children is requested. One mile beyond the Paradise Point Audubon Nature Center at the junction of NH 3A is Six Chimneys Bed and Breakfast (described in the introduction of this tour) where you might want to stop, making this a leisurely two-day tour.

Wellington State Park, to your left on West Side Road 4.3 miles south of Hebron, is a welcome spot for hot, weary cyclists. The park offers swimming in Newfound Lake and picnicking facilities. There are also twelve different hiking trails should you desire a respite from your bicycle seat.

Hebron Village Store, adjacent to the green, is open all day, every day and sells cold cuts and sandwiches in addition to groceries.

West Shore Road is a narrow, two-lane road over rolling to hilly terrain with limited visibility. In summer, caution is urged because of heavy traffic. However, the speed limit is only twenty and thirty miles per hour along this stretch, so cyclists are safe on this route.

29.2   At the stop sign, turn right towards Alexandria and follow the main road 1.2 miles.

From West Shore Road to Alexandria and on to NH 104, the roads tend to be typical of backcountry New Hampshire: winding and rolling with poor to fair surface and no shoulders.

30.4   Turn sharply left by the sign for Alexandria and ride 1 mile into the village. Stay with the main road as it turns right to head out of the village and then bends left to a fork. There are no shops in the village of Alexandria.

31.4   At the fork, bear left onto the road marked for Danbury and ride 3.5 miles to NH 104.

34.9   When you reach NH 104, turn right and ride 5.5 miles to US 4 and the center of Danbury.

NH 104 is a wide road with paved shoulders for 2.5 miles, good visibility, and fast traffic. The remaining 3 miles offer a good surface, but the shoulder turns to gravel and the roadway tends to be curvy.

The Inn at Danbury with its bicycle shop, described in the introduction to this tour, is located at 40.1 miles on the left.

40.4   In Danbury, turn right onto US 4 and bike for 14.1 miles through the Graftons back to Canaan.

Because US 4 is fairly open, you have good views of the countryside and mountains along this stretch. The road to the Ruggles Mine, an old mine worth visiting, leaves from Grafton Center (there's a sign to direct you). However, we suggest you do not attempt the difficult ride up the steep grades on your bicycle. The road is very narrow and poorly surfaced, and the side trip is better made by automobile.

There are two food stores in Danbury at the junction of NH 104 and US 4. Dick's General Store and Danbury General Store are both open all day, every day. Maynard's Country Store on US 4 in Grafton 7.6 miles from its junction with NH 104 is also open all day, every day. You can buy steamed hot dogs and hot coffee here as well as groceries.

US 4 is level to rolling, with good visibility, a smooth surface, and a gravel shoulder. While it is considered a major route, traffic is usually light due to the presence of I-89 just to the south.

54.5   You are in Canaan, your starting point.

13

Hanover-Orford

36.6 miles; moderate cycling
Rolling terrain

Hanover is the cultural and educational center of northwestern New Hampshire. Home of Dartmouth College, the Hopkins Center for the Performing Arts, and Mary Hitchcock Medical Center, it is a beehive of activity. Stately, ivy-covered college buildings, wide lawns bordering tree-lined streets, and the Hanover Inn overlooking an expansive village green lend a feeling of tradition and stability to the town. At the same time book-laden college students bustling between classes and the presence of numerous specialty shops catering to a diversity of interests and needs convey a sense of excitement and dynamism.

Yet, within five minutes of leaving town on this tour you are cycling amidst the farms, pastures, and corn fields of the northern Connecticut River Valley. While such a contrast results in momentary culture shock, the transition is a pleasant one to which you happily adapt. The cycling is generally easy, and the scenery often magnificent. The tour is classified as a moderate trip primarily because of its length, and we suggest you make it an all-day affair, allotting ample time for exploring the towns of Lyme and Orford. Also budget time for a picnic lunch along the bank of the Connecticut River, which you follow on your return from Orford. Slowly snaking its way between the round-topped hills of eastern Vermont and the foothills of New Hampshire's White Mountains, its serenity is contagious. With any luck at all, you'll return to Hanover relaxed, refreshed, and ready for a good dinner to end a perfect day.

Several inns, located along your route, provide warmth and comfort should you decide to complement your day of cycling with an overnight stay. Each is noted in the tour description.

This trip begins by the Hanover Inn near the Dartmouth College green. While there are parking spaces available here, they are usually full, so you may want to head for nearby side streets or municipal lots.

0.0   From the green, follow East Wheelock Street, which is also NH 10, past the Hanover Inn and the Hopkins Center a couple of blocks to a traffic light. To stay on NH 10, turn left here and then right at the next traffic light. Continue north on NH 10 for 10.7 miles to Lyme.

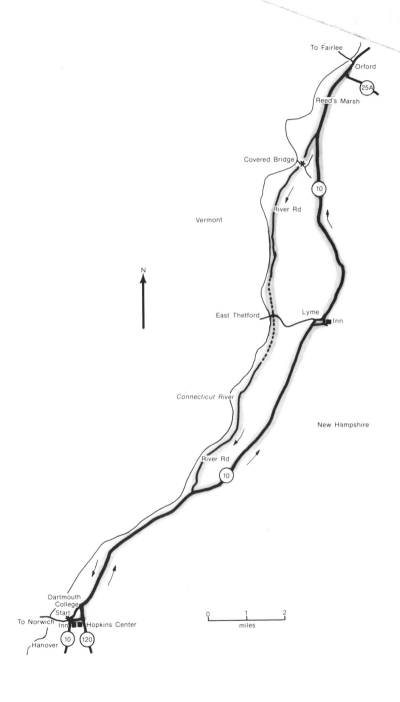

To Fairlee

Orford

25A

Reed's Marsh

Covered Bridge

10

River Rd

Vermont

N

East Thetford

Lyme

Inn

Connecticut River

New Hampshire

River Rd

10

Dartmouth College

Start

To Norwich

Inn

Hopkins Center

10 120

Hanover

0   1   2
miles

Dartmouth College, the Hopkins Center, and the town of Hanover offer a variety of activities too numerous to list here. For up-to-date information, call the Hopkins Center at 646-2422.

You can purchase food at P&C Grocery (8–9 Mon.–Sat., 8–6 Sun.) on the main street (NH 10) of Hanover. It also has a large deli where you can purchase sandwiches and hot food. You can also buy groceries and deli food at Pat and Tony's General Store on NH 10 0.8 mile north of the second traffic light.

Hanover has a number of enjoyable places to eat. Peter Christian's Tavern (11:30–12:30 daily), Molly's Delicatessen (8:30–5 Mon.–Sat.), and 5 Olde Nugget Alley (11–11:30 Mon.–Sat.; Sunday brunch 10:30–2, dinner 4:30–11) are a few of your choices. All three are located on Main Street.

The Hanover Inn (643-4300) on the green in downtown Hanover is a stately brick building with nicely appointed lobby and rooms. Across the Connecticut River on Main Street in Norwich, Vermont, is the Inn at Norwich (649-1143), established in 1797.

NH 10 is a wide, smooth road with excellent shoulders. While traffic tends to be considerable in town, it thins out as you head north. The wide, paved shoulders provide ample room for cycling outside the traffic lanes. The terrain is hilly, but the roadway is well graded, resulting in more gradual slopes than might be expected. Visibility is excellent, and there are numerous expansive views of the Connecticut River and mountains and farms in both New Hampshire and Vermont.

10.7 In Lyme, bear sharply right off NH 10 onto the road that edges the right side of the long town common. At the head of the common turn left, in front of the Lyme Inn, and take the road between the church and horse sheds to a yield sign, where you rejoin NH 10. Continue north another 7.3 miles to Orford.

Lyme's Congregational Church was built in 1812 and its horse sheds are a rare example of original meeting house outbuildings. The Lyme Inn, (603/795-2222) built between 1802 and 1809, is a small, intimate country inn where area literati and artists often gather on Sunday afternoons for readings and discussions. It has fifteen rooms and serves dinner daily except Tuesday. Reservations for lodging and dinner are suggested.

In Lyme you can purchase lunch or a snack at the counter in Nichol's Hardware (7:30–5:30 Mon.–Sat.) or groceries and sandwiches at the Lyme Country Store (8–8 Mon.–Sat., 9–6 Sun.). Carol's Country Store (9–8 daily), located 4.3 miles north of Lyme, sells sandwiches and groceries.

After you leave Lyme, NH 10 narrows and the shoulder, when it exists at all, is loose gravel. However, visibility remains excellent, and there are fewer hills. While traffic is generally light to moderate, it is also fast moving; we urge you to be careful.

18.5   At the red brick church in Orford, turn around and retrace your route 2.7
miles to a fork in the road.

In Orford, you should note the seven "ridge" houses: built between 1773
and 1839, they display the influence of architects Charles Bulfinch and
Asher Benjamin. Orford was also the home of Samuel Morey, who was
credited with the invention of America's first marine steam engine,
predating Robert Fulton's 1803 boat by nearly ten years.

The White Goose Inn (353-4812) located 0.9 mile south of Orford,
is a meticulously refurbished brick structure that was built in 1833. With
beautifully decorated parlor, guestrooms, and dining room, it creates
a special atmosphere for guests who wish to enjoy its bed and breakfast accommodations. The innkeepers do not serve lunch and dinner.

Food can be purchased at the Orford General Store (8–8
Mon.–Sat., 9–6 Sun.). You won't see any more restaurants or stores
until your return to the outskirts of Hanover.

21.2   At the fork, bear right off NH 10 and ride for 5.3 miles, through the Lyme-
Edgell covered bridge, to a stop sign.

Within minutes of leaving Hanover, you are cycling amidst pastoral scenes such as
this one.

Reed's Marsh, a New Hampshire wildlife management area located just south of Orford and adjacent to the Connecticut River, supports a variety of bird, animal, and fish species. The Lyme–Edgell covered bridge, constructed in 1885 by Walter and J.C. Piper, is 154 feet long and crosses Clay Brook. The countryside around this backroad is mostly corn fields and pastureland. A way unlikely to be discovered by the passing tourist, it is always close to the river and affords some great views.

Although the backroads along the river are often cracked and bumpy, they are quite ridable. They are narrow with no shoulders, but have very little traffic. Note that 3.8 miles after you turn off NH 10 the road turns to gravel for 1 mile. However, it is hardpacked, wide, and level, so it should present no problem.

26.5   At the stop sign and crossroad that leads to the right, over the river, to Vermont, continue straight another 5.4 miles before rejoining NH 10.

31.9   Turn right onto NH 10 and retrace the rest of your route for 4.7 miles back to Hanover.

36.6   You are back at your starting point in front of the Hanover Inn.

Bicycle Repair Services

Omer and Bob's Ski, Tennis and Bike Shop, Nugget Arcade, Hanover (643-3525).
Peddler Bike Shop, 5 Allen St., Hanover (643-5271).

Concord Area

14

Concord-Hopkinton

14.1 miles; easy cycling
Level to rolling terrain, with several short hills

Offering an excellent introduction to the world of cycle touring, our Concord-Hopkinton trip couples easy biking along little traveled roads with convenient access to New Hampshire's capitol. In fact, although about half the tour is within Concord's city limits, the roads you travel there take you past several ponds and farms as well as the campus of St. Paul's School. Just over fourteen miles long, the tour is ideal for a morning or afternoon jaunt and is particularly suited for introducing the family to bicycle touring. You are also treated to the pleasure of a traffic-free ride along a bicycle path which parallels I-89 for 1.4 miles. Built at the same time as I-89, it was constructed to provide access for bicyclists, pedestrians, and St. Paul's students to Turkey Pond, which was cut off from the campus when the highway was built. The path also functions as a convenient connector between a network of lightly traveled rural roads. For information on local accommodations in the Concord and Henniker areas consult our Shaker Village and Crotched Mountain–Colby Hill tours.

We suggest you start adjacent to Exit 3 (Stickney Hill Road) of I-89, approximately four miles northwest of the intersection of I-89 and I-93 south of Concord. A short access road on the south side of I-89 leads left off Stickney Hill Road to a bicycle path. Park along the side of this access road and begin your trip.

0.0 From your starting point, Stickney Hill Road is a smoothly surfaced road for one mile. For the last two miles it is narrow, bumpy and nearly free of traffic. Much of it is shaded by a tunnel of tree branches, offering cool cycling on hot summer days. There is one short, steep upgrade at the beginning of the tour followed by a very gradual rise to Jewett Road.

While there are no specific points of interest along this rural section, you pass several attractive farms and homes.

3.0 Turn right at Jewett Road and ride 0.6 mile, over the interstate, to US 202/NH 9/NH 103.

Boulder Farm, located at the intersection of US 202/NH 9/NH 103 and Jewett Road, produces many acres of strawberries. If you take this tour in June or early July you can treat yourself to a feast and "pick your own."

3.6   Turn left and ride for 1.1 miles through the center of Hopkinton to the general store, The Cracker Barrel, at the west end of town. Here NH 103 diverges to the right from US 202/NH 9 toward Contoocook.

The main street of Hopkinton is worth a leisurely visit to view the beautiful colonials, large white churches, and impressive town hall, all set back from a roadway lined with magnificent shade trees. St. Andrew's Church on the village common, built in 1827-1828 and designed by architect John Leach, is of Granite Ashlar construction, a style typical of New England Episcopal churches in the period.

The Cracker Barrel is a well stocked country store (8–6 Mon.–Sat., 8–3 Sun.).

Kimball's Lakeside Restaurant and Lounge and the Horseshoe Tavern, adjacent establishments in the town of Hopkinton on US 202/NH 9/NH 103 0.5 mile west of Jewett Road, are two very nice places to eat. Kimball's (11:30–9 daily, 746-4171) features lunches from $2.50, dinners from $5.50, a buffet for $6.00 and a salad bar. The Horseshoe Tavern (5–9 Wed.–Sat., 11–8 Sun., 746-4501) offers "elegant country dining." Both are located in very pleasant surroundings overlooking Smith Pond.

US 202/NH 9/NH 103 is a wide, two-lane road with no shoulder. Since this section of road is near an interchange with I-89, it tends to have more traffic than other sections of the route. However, road visibility is good and the speed limit is low in the center of Hopkinton. The terrain is generally flat.

4.7   From The Cracker Barrel, retrace your route for 1.1 miles to the junction of Jewett Road. Continue east on US 202/NH 9/NH 103 an additional 1.5 miles to an unmarked road on the left. Note Whittier Pond on your left just before the turn.

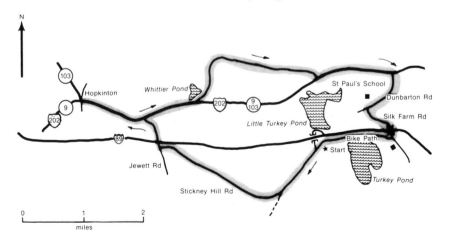

Finders Keepers Antiques, Etc., is located on US 202/NH 9/NH 103 just east of Jewett Road.

Here US 202/NH 9/NH 103 is wide with no shoulder and a new surface. In spite of being three highways sharing one roadway, it is reasonably safe road to cycle since many people tend to use I-89. For most of your 1.5 miles on this road you will encounter light to moderate traffic, and you'll be descending as you leave Hopkinton.

7.3   By Whittier Pond, turn left and follow the unmarked road for 2.6 miles until it rejoins the main highway.

Narrow, with a good surface, no shoulder, and well-shaded, this side road offers you a gentle downhill run away from the rush of traffic.

9.9   At the junction with US 202/NH 9/NH 103, turn left and ride 1.2 miles to Dunbarton Road, which is also the entrance to St. Paul's School.

The numbered highway remains wide with no shoulder and moderate traffic. Here you can coast most of the first mile, but there is a short uphill grade just before your next turn.

11.1   At Dunbarton Road, turn right and ride 0.8 mile to Silk Farm Road, on your left.

St. Paul's School, a private, coeducational, secondary school, is situated on 1,800 acres of woods and open land. Its manicured grounds

The cyclist's dream: an effortless descent alongside well-kept stone walls and open fields.

and attractive buildings entice you to stop for a rest, or at least a look.
Dunbarton Road has a smooth surface, no shoulder, and very light traffic. The terrain is nearly level.

11.9   At Silk Farm Road, turn left and ride another 0.8 mile, passing under I-89, where the bicycle path leads off to the right.
Audubon House (9–5 Mon.–Fri., 9–3 Sun.) is located on Silk Farm Road 0.2 mile beyond the entrance to the bicycle path. Headquarters of the New Hampshire Audubon Society, it features a gift shop, library, and two short nature paths.
Silk Farm Road is similar to Dunbarton Road.

12.7   Immediately beyond the I-89 underpass, turn right onto the paved bicycle path, which parallels the interstate highway for 1.4 miles.
The bicycle path offers an excellent eight-foot-wide surface and no motorized traffic.

14.1   You are back at your start at the other end of the bicycle path.

15

Dunbarton-Goffstown

22.5 miles, Hilly

Situated between the cities of Concord and Manchester, the Dunbarton/Goffstown trip offers southern New Hampshire and Boston area cyclists quick, easy access to the rural beauty and backroad touring of the Granite State. It is pleasantly surprising how quickly the urban environment of Manchester, the state's largest city, gives way to the small towns, hamlets, and country livin' that predominates on this tour. Set up in a figure eight pattern, this trip is relatively short, and we have purposely kept it that way because it is quite hilly. Pains were taken to plan the route with a lot of descents to offset the groans of hill climbs, and anyone who is even moderately fit should experience no serious difficulty with it. However, a good granny gear would serve you well and help to flatten out the upward pulls, most of which are gradual. And there are rewards for your efforts! Besides enjoying some long descents, you will see sweeping views of southern New Hampshire along NH 13. Clough State Park has swimming and picnicking in the summer months. Dunbarton offers a glimpse of traditional New England architecture with its town hall, Congregational Church and assorted white frame buildings. Finally, Goffstown, with its old victorian and colonial homes and several good places to eat, is a spot to enjoy a break midway through the tour.

The tour begins at Dunbarton Country Store located at the junction of NH 13 and Winslow Road in Dunbarton. To get there follow NH 13 for 5 miles south from the I-89 overpass in Concord or take NH 13 north for 8.6 miles from its junction with NH 114 in Goffstown. Park along Winslow Road. Dunbarton Country Store (7–8 Mon.–Sat., 8–8 Sun.), in addition to regular groceries, has a deli with a good assortment of fresh sandwiches.

0.0 Start this tour by following Winslow Road/Stark Lane for 1.5 miles to its junction with Mansion Road.

Winslow Road is a shoulderless two lane road which rises and dips frequently. Note the fork after 0.8 mile: bear left at this junction which becomes Stark Lane (unmarked).

After immediately going through a bog area, the road passes through a heavily wooded section including Dunbarton Town Forest.

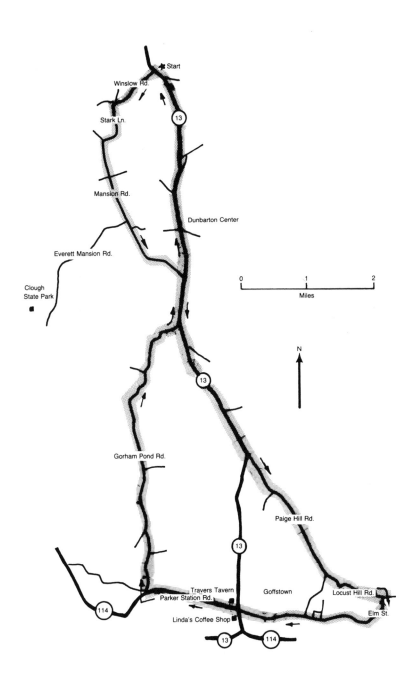

1.5   Turn left on Mansion Road and ride 2.5 miles to the junction with NH 13. Mansion Road a two lane road of the same quality as Winslow Road and Stark Lane. It rises gradually most of the way to NH 13, then it ascends rather steeply for 0.7 mile just before joining NH 13.

At 2.8 miles you come to the junction of Mansion Road and Everett Mansion Road with clearly marked signs to Clough State Park and Everett Dam. Should you wish to picnic and swim at Clough State Park or take a look at Everett Dam, which is part of the Hopkinton Everett Flood Control Area, turn right on Everett Mansion Road and ride 1.25 miles to these facilities.

4.0   Turn right and proceed for 3 miles to an unmarked road on the left side of NH 13 in the middle of a sharp right hand curve.

NH 13, wider than Mansion Road with a smooth surface and light to moderate traffic, ascends gradually for 1.8 miles to Goffstown Country Club, the highest point on the trip, and then descends for 0.8 mile. There are beautiful views to the south and west on this section.

Goffstown Country Club (774-5031) is open to the public and has a snack bar open during daylight hours overlooking the beautiful 9th fairway.

7.0   Turn left onto the unmarked road, Paige Hill Road, and follow it for 2.2 miles to a fork. Take the left fork, Locust Hill Road, and ride 1 mile to its junction with Elm Street.

Paige Hill Road is a narrow two lane road with no shoulder and varying surface conditions from smooth to sections with frost heaves. It is all quite ridable and traffic is normally very light. With the exception of a slight rise of 0.2 mile, this whole section descends gradually, then steeply, so enjoy!

Round Wheel Orchard, where you can buy fruit in season, is located on the left at 8.2 miles.

10.2   Turn right on Elm Street and ride 2.5 miles to the junction of Elm Street with NH 114 and NH 13.

Elm Street is about as wide and smooth as NH 13 and carries moderate traffic as it connects Goffstown with Manchester. With the exception of a short ascent of 0.2 mile as soon as you turn onto Elm Street, the road stays mostly level as it approaches Goffstown along the banks of the Piscataquog River.

At 11.1 miles there is a sandy beach area with a sign indicating "Swim at your own risk as per order of selectmen."

Travers Tavern (lunch 11:30–2, dinner 5:30–10 Tues.–Sat., call 497-3978 for reservations) is a very nice restaurant located on NH 13 just a few hundred feet from the junction of Elm Street, NH 114 and NH 13. Serving a continental menu, it caters more to the leisurely diner than to sweaty cyclists clad in bike shorts and Tee shirts. But it offers a nice beginning or end to a day of cycling when you can arrive in more suitable clothing.

Linda's Coffee Shop and Bakery (5–6 Mon.–Thurs., 5–8 Fri. and Sat., 5–3 Sun, 497-2222) is better suited to a weary cyclist with a big appetite and insatiable sweet tooth. Located on the Main Street (NH 114) of Goffstown just a few yards to the left of the junction of Elm Street and NH 114, it features inexpensive daily specials and a nice assortment of baked goods.

12.7 Turn right followed by an immediate left onto NH 114 north (also called North Mast Road) and ride 1.3 miles to Parker Station Road. Turn right, ride 0.1 mile to Gorham Pond Road. Turn right again and ride 4.3 miles to the junction of NH 13.

NH 114 is a two-lane road with moderate traffic. After 0.6 mile there is a paved shoulder. Nice old colonials and victorian homes grace this section of town. Lyon's Handweaving, open by appointment or by chance, is situated on NH 114 at the corner of Clinton Street.

Gorham Pond Road is a narrow two lane road through pleasant country. It rises gradually all the way to NH 114.

The Goffstown Historical Society is located at the corner of Parker Station Road and Gorham Pond Road.

18.4 Turn left on NH 13 and ride 4.1 miles back to Dunbarton Country Store. From Gorham Pond Road to Mansion Road, a distance of 0.7 mile, you are duplicating a section of NH 13 ridden earlier in the day.

Gentle curves, grazing cattle and an unhurried cyclist.

At 19.8 miles you are in the village of Dunbarton with its traditional New England architecture.

At 20.8 begin a steep 1.7 mile descent to end your day.

22.5   Your tour ends at Dunbarton Country Store.

16
Shaker Village

26.0 miles; moderate terrain
Several short, steep hills

In 1792, a celibate religious community from Manchester, England, known as the Shakers, established a community of converts on the farm of Benjamin Whitcher in Canterbury, NH. At its height in 1850, the community consisted of 250 converts operating a commercial agricultural system of 6,000 acres with 100 buildings, including dwellings, workshops, barns, and water-powered mills. Remaining today are twenty-two buildings demonstrating their architecture and housing the furniture and crafts of these gifted people. Guided tours, a gift shop, and a restaurant serving traditional Shaker food are available. This village is the focal point of the tour which begins and ends in Concord, the capital of New Hampshire. Offering moderate terrain, low traffic, and very appealing views of the Merrimack Valley Region, it is a trip which should particularly appeal to families with young aspiring cyclists and also to history buffs who need an intellectual justification for a bike ride.

You may wish to avoid this tour during the third weekend in June when thousands of motorcyclists invade Loudon Speedway on NH 106 for the Loudon Classic Motorcycle race, the oldest race of its kind in the U.S.

For those who wish to make a weekend of it, Concord is a pleasant city with a small town atmosphere. While there are no country inns within its environs, a number of motels provide suitable accommodations, including the Brick Tower Motor Inn (224-9565), Concord Coach Motor Inn (224-2511), Howard Johnson's (224-4011), New Hampshire Highway Motel (225-6687), and the Ramada Inn (224-9534). Eagle Square, a recently renovated downtown mall, has many small boutiques, shops and restaurants. The Durgen Block, scheduled for completion late in 1985, will add more of the same. A city on the move, Concord is doing much to renovate its downtown areas while private developers and homeowners continue to refurbish the city's fine old victorian houses. Several downtown restaurants serving a variety of fine food include Tio Juan's (Mexican), Thursday's (crepes, quiches, breads, soups), Osgood's (traditional), B. Mae Denny's (informal in-town eating), and The Millstone (traditional). For gourmets on the move try Anthron's Fine Food and Take Out at 9 Depot Street, which features summer and fall picnic baskets.

The tour begins in the parking lot of the Bradlee's/Market Basket Shopping Center on Fort Eddy Road in Concord. To get to the starting point, follow I-93 to I-393 (Exit 15-E). Take the first exit off I-393 marked Fort Eddy Road/New Hampshire Technical Institute. At the T-intersection at the end of the exit ramp, turn right and proceed for 0.3 mile to the entrance to the shopping center on the left.

0.0   From the shopping center, turn right and ride 0.2 mile along Fort Eddy Road to a bicycle path located on the left side of the road just beyond Funspot. Follow the bicycle path 0.1 mile under I-393 to its junction with the New Hampshire Technical Institute Fire Access Road. Follow the access road through NHTI grounds for 0.5 mile to its junction with Fan Road (unmarked). Turn left and ride for about 50 yards to a bike path which begins on the right of Fan Road just before the bridge over I-93. Take the bike path for 0.5 mile to its junction with Eastman Street in East Concord. Follow Eastman Street for 0.4 mile to its junction with NH 132, East Side Drive.

Food is available at the Market Basket and also at Brookfield market on Eastman Street.

Aside from Fort Eddy Road, traffic should be very light on this section of the trip.

Note the historical monument on Eastman Road commemorating Captain Ebenezer Eastman, first settler of Concord in 1727, who established the first ferry in the same year on this site.

1.7   Bear left on NH 132 north, also known as Mountain Road, and ride for 6.4 miles to an unmarked road on the right noted by a sign directing you to Canterbury Center and Shaker Village.

Bridges House, the official governor's residence, is located on the left side of NH 132, 0.2 mile north of the Eastman Street intersection. This brick colonial was built in 1836 and donated to the state by Styles Bridges, former Governor of New Hampshire and U.S. Senator.

NH 132 is a two lane road with a smooth surface, no shoulder, and generally low traffic. It has several short steep hills, especially near Concord Country Club at 2.9 miles, but usually it rolls moderately.

Open westerly views of the Merrimack Valley can be seen at 3.3 miles just beyond Blye Farm Condominiums.

8.1   At the intersection of NH 132 and the road to Canterbury Center, turn right and proceed 1.1 miles to the junction of Baptist Road in Canterbury Center. Note that there is a T-intersection after 0.4 mile. Bear left and continue to Canterbury Center.

Kimball Pond Conservation Area is located on the left after 0.5 mile.

The road surface is not as smooth as NH 132 but it is very ridable. There is no shoulder but traffic is light. A steep hill, 0.2 mile long, is located just beyond Kimball Pond.

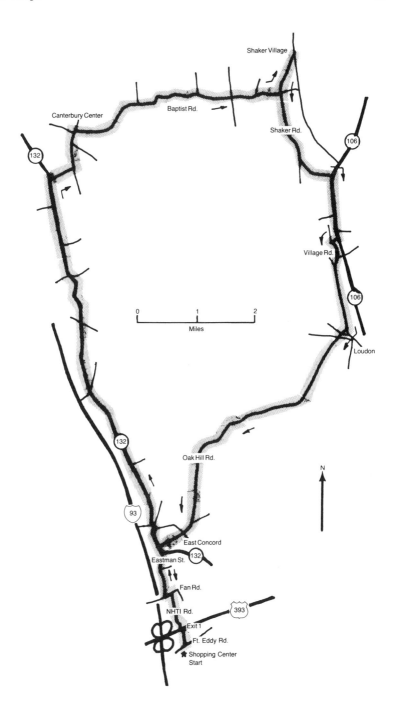

9.2   Turn right on Baptist Road (unmarked) and ride 3.7 miles to its junction with Shaker Road (unmarked). There is a sign at this intersection directing you to Shaker Village and Loudon.

The picturesque Village of Canterbury Center has a town hall, church, library and general store, which offers an opportunity for a rest stop or snack.

Baptist Road has some short, steep ascents and descents. The road's surface, although adequate for riding, has frost heaves, and sometimes crates a washboard effect. The area is wooded with occasional bogs. You will also see several nicely restored houses.

12.9   Turn left on Shaker Road and ride 1 mile to Shaker Village.

Shaker Village is open Tuesday through Saturday and holiday Mondays, from mid-May through Mid-October, 10–5. Knowledgeable guides, who interpret 200 years of Shaker history, lead hour-long walking tours of six historical buildings. Craftsmen offer demonstrations in Shaker basket making, tinsmithing, woodworking and sewing.

The Creamery (10–4:30, lunch 11:30–3), a building where cream and butter were once made, serves traditional Shaker meals at moderate prices which vary from $1.95 to $5.95. There is also a picnic area for those who choose to bring a lunch.

13.9   After a visit to Shaker Village retrace your route south on Shaker Road for 1 mile, but continue straight ahead for another 1.7 miles to the junction of NH 106 in Loudon instead of taking Baptist Road back to Canterbury Center.

The Beanstalk General Store is located on the left side of Shaker Road at the junction of NH 106.

16.6   Turn right and head south on NH 106 for exactly 1 mile to Village Road. NH 106 is a two lane road with a wide, paved shoulder, smooth surface and moderate traffic.

17.6   Turn right on Village Road, which makes an immediate sharp left, and follow it through a populated residential and commercial area for 1.5 miles to Oak Hill Road on the right.

19.1   Turn right on Oak Hill Road, follow it straight through two intersections and continue for 5.2 miles to its junction with NH 132, Mountain Road. Note that the name Oak Hill Road changes to Shawmut Road at its junction with NH 132.

Oak Hill Road is a two lane shoulderless road with light to moderate traffic. It offers a fair surface which improves when you cross the line into Concord. There is a gradual climb of 0.6 mile shortly after turning on Oak Hill Road followed by a gradual descent all the way to NH 132.

Loudon Village Antiques is located on Oak Hill Road 0.1 mile beyond its junction with Village Road. According to the proprietor, a retired gentleman who lives there, it is open "most of the time" or by

The Bandstand—another traditional New England fixture to be seen in many New Hampshire villages.

appointment (783-4741).

At the top of the 0.6 mile climb there are excellent views of Concord and Turtletown Pond. For the ambitious there is a 2-mile walk to the Oak Hill Lookout Tower.

As you descend towards Concord you will pass a number of beautiful country houses as well as Turtletown Pond Conservation Area.

24.3 Turn left on NH 132, pass the Exxon Station, take an immediate right on Eastman Street and retrace your route 1.7 miles.

26.0 Return to Bradlee's/Market Basket Shopping Center, your starting point.

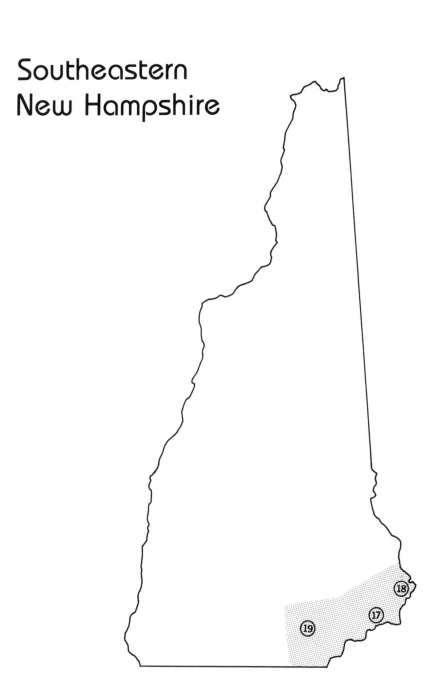

Southeastern
New Hampshire

17
Exeter

28.5 miles; easy cycling
Level to rolling terrain

Here, cycling across the gently rolling terrain of New Hampshire's coastal plain, you are free to absorb the vistas that unfold before you, for there are few hills and little traffic to distract you on this route. A curve in the road may bring into view a tiny hamlet, an open expanse of pastureland, country-suburban residences, or the campus of one of America's most respected academies. Never strictly rural in nature, this trip begins in the bustling town of Exeter not far from the buildings of famed Phillips Exeter Academy and then loops south through attractive countryside, dipping briefly into neighboring Massachusetts. It is hard to image that this region sits on the edge of a major urban complex, for although the deep woods and mountains that characterize so much of New Hampshire are missing, there is still much open farmland and newer homes are well spaced. Particularly appealing are the acres of apple orchards with row upon row of trees brightly colored with blossoms in late spring and heavily laden with fruit in fall. But whatever the season, the roads, towns, countryside, and terrain of this region combine to offer a pleasant day of easy riding.

Your trip starts at the foot of Front Street in the center of Exeter, by the town hall and bandstand. Parking is available here and throughout the town.

0.0 From the bandstand, turn right onto Water Street (NH 108). After 0.2 mile, NH 108 bears off to the left; your route continues straight on US 101C/NH 88 toward Hampton.

Although Exeter's roots are firmly planted in its seventeenth-century past, its townsfolk have managed to accommodate the change brought about by twentieth-century demands while preserving many of the historical landmarks. Because the many famous men who have lived in this town left their mark, there are a number of significant historical sites to visit. If you have time to explore the town, pick up the booklet of walking tours printed by the Exeter Historical Society. Also highly recommended is a tour of Phillips Exeter Academy, whose impact on the community has been considerable since its founding in 1781. Many of its buildings are open to the public.

Lodging is available in Exeter at the Exeter Inn, 90 Front Street, on the campus of Phillips Exeter Academy. It features Georgian architecture and a traditional dining room and cocktail lounge (772-5901). The Loaf and Ladle, 9 Water Street offers informal dining, good food and reasonable prices (11–8 daily except Sunday, 778-8955). The Epicurean & Fox & Hounds Pub, 48 Portsmouth Avenue, features steaks, seafood, soups, sandwiches and quiche (lunch daily 11:30–4, dinner daily 5–9, 772-9300).

Wheel Power, a bicycle shop on Water Street, located across the street from the bandstand, is open Monday through Saturday, 9:30–5:30.

The route from Exeter to Hampton Falls is a winding country road along which houses are scattered. The surface is rather rough, but the roadway is level and bears little traffic.

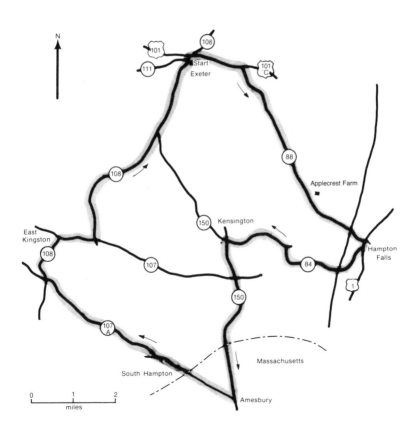

1.3   At the fork where US 101C bears left to Hampton, bear right on NH 88
for 5.6 miles to a T-junction in Hampton Falls.
The 500-acre Applecrest Farm, 5.0 miles from Exeter, supports over
twenty thousand apple trees, as well as smaller orchards of other fruit
trees and some vegetable gardens. Fruit and produce, cider, maple
syrup, home-baked breads and pastries, cheese and other items are
sold at the farm's roadside store, Applecrest Applemart, on NH 88. In
season you may pick your own fruit if you wish. As you come into Hampton Falls, note the quaint Unitarian Meeting House and then the Baptist Church, locally called the "Beer Bottle Church" because it is topped
by a wooden copy of a beer bottle.
In addition to the goodies available at Applecrest Applemart, food
is available at the R.P. Merrill and Son General Store in Hampton Falls.

6.9   At the junction in Hampton Falls, turn right onto US 1/NH 84 and then immediately right again onto the road signposted "Kensington." This is NH
84 (it is not so marked here), which you follow for 4.3 miles to NH 150 on
the outskirts of Kensington.
NH 84 is a narrow, twisting, but level road. After taking you through
a small residential area, it breaks into open countryside where there
is little traffic.

11.2   At the junction, turn sharply left onto NH 150, continue straight across NH
107, and ride for 3.9 miles over the state line and into thickly settled Amesbury, Massachusetts.
If you want cold drinks, hot coffee, or snacks, watch for Pete's Variety
on the right as you enter Amesbury.
NH 150 is wider than NH 84 and has gravel shoulders, good visibility, and light to moderate traffic. The terrain is more rolling than that
over which you have just ridden.

15.1   In Amesbury watch carefully for your next turn, as there are no town signs
or route numbers to give you warning. As you come into the heavily residential section of Amesbury on a slight down grade, there will be a small trian-
gular common with a granite war memorial in the center of it. At this point,
make a very sharp right turn onto South Hampton Road, which becomes
NH 107A as soon as it crosses the New Hampshire line. Continue on this
road 6 miles, through South Hampton, to NH 108.
This stretch of NH 107A is a two-lane road with no shoulder, light traffic,
and good visibility. There is one gradual climb to South Hampton, which
is followed by a downgrade. The rest of the route is quite level.

21.1   At the junction, turn right onto NH 108 and ride 1.1 miles to the stop sign
in East Kingston.
At the stop sign in East Kingston, Poggio General Store is in sight on
your left. A food store with deli, their hours are all day every day except Sunday when it opens at 10 AM.

22.2 In East Kingston, turn right onto NH 107/NH 108 toward Exeter for 0.9 mile.

23.1 At the fork where NH 107 continues straight, bear left to stay on NH 108, which brings you back to Exeter in 5.4 miles.

NH 108 back to Exeter has a smooth surface, no shoulder, and moderate traffic. The terrain is level to rolling.

28.5 At the yield sign in Exeter where NH 111 comes in from the left and US 101/NH 108 breaks off to the right, turn right onto Front Street to reach your point of departure.

Bicycle Repair Services
Wheel Power, Water St., Exeter (772-6343).

There are few hills and surprisingly little traffic on the winding roads the Exeter tour follows.

18

Portsmouth-Little Boars Head

32.0 miles; easy cycling
Level to slightly rolling terrain

New Hampshire can lay claim to only a few miles of Atlantic coastline, but that short distance makes up in variety what it lacks in length. Here you find pounding surf, fine sandy beaches, and rocky cliffs; salt marshes and small harbors; old forts and old villages; and, in summer particularly, people. Because the sun and sea exert such a powerful attraction, you may encounter considerable traffic on this trip, especially on summer weekends. Consequently, we strongly suggest that you venture here only during mid-week in summer or preferably in late spring or early fall, when there is ample warmth, solitude, and space for an exhilarating ride.

Cruise along the winding road that parallels the shoreline and enjoy the great expanses of ocean views. On clear days, the Isle of Shoals lighthouse is visible over ten miles offshore, and you can often see freighters or sailing boats on the horizon. In addition to providing recreation, the ocean is still an avenue of travel, just as it was when early settlers found their way in 1623 to this shore's safe harbors. Much of the region's early history is preserved in numerous historical sites along the route, the most notable of which is Portsmouth's Strawbery Banke. This trip also takes you inland a short way through open, level farmland with weathered homes and barns. It is an ideal outing for those who wish to couple easy cycling with a generous diversity of potential activities.

There are many inns and lodges in the Portsmouth area. Several that you can try include: The Anchorage Motor Inn (431-8111), Howard Johnson's (436-2700), and The Port Motor Inn (436-4378), all located near Exit 5 off I-95 at the Portsmouth Traffic Circle. The Inn at Christian Shore, 335 Maplewood Avenue (431-6770) is close to downtown while the Pebble Beach Motel (431-5896) is on the ocean near Odiorne State Park.

Portsmouth also has many fine restaurants. One of the most famous is the Blue Strawbery, 29 Ceres Street (431-6420) which features a 9-item 6-course dinner with seatings at 6 and 9 PM. Reservations are required for this $28.00 feast. There are also many other restaurants to choose from in the vicinity of Ceres and Bow Streets including the Dolphin Striker, Tumbledowns, The Old Ferry Landing and Poco Diablo for those who like Mexican food. The Tavern at Strawbery Banke (431-2816) at the corner of Marcy and Court Streets, across from Prescott Park, features a Sunday Brunch 11–4. Except for Monday, when it is closed, lunch is served 11:30–2 and dinner 5:30–10. For those who wish to combine cycling with other pleasurable activities, consider attending a play at the Theatre by the Sea near the junction of Route 1 and Bow Street.

To reach the tour's start in the Strawbery Banke area of Portsmouth, follow the small strawberry signs posted along major routes into town. Parking is usually available on side streets around the Banke, or in the municipal lot next to Prescott Park; the lot's entrance is by the corner of Marcy and

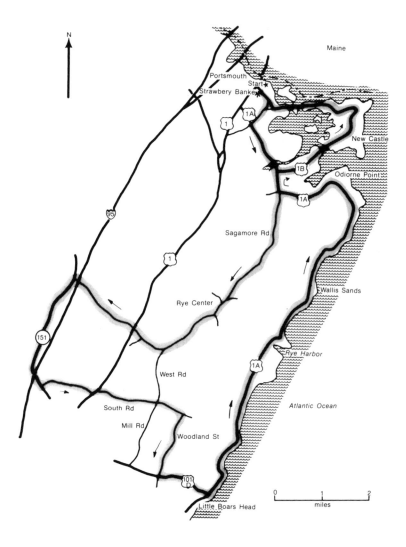

State streets, adjacent to the old drawbridge to Kittery, Maine.

0.0   From the parking lot, turn left onto Marcy Street and cycle 0.4 mile to its end at a four-way intersection.

You pass the entrance to Strawbery Banke, a ten-acre museum that contains more than thirty buildings dating from the seventeenth, eighteenth, and nineteenth centuries. The grounds are open from May 1 to October 31. The lawns and gardens of Prescott Park, across the street from the Banke's entrance and stretching to the piers along the Piscataqua River, are the setting for an annual summer-long arts festival of plays and concerts, among other events.

Marcy Street is an old narrow, winding city street.

0.4   At the intersection, continue straight on South Street, passing the Blue Fin fish market on the left and following the signs to Hampton and Rye. Continue straight through two blinking lights to a traffic light at the junction of US 1A.

You pass Marconi's Grocery, on the right, on South Street. South Street is similar to Marcy, but slightly wider.

1.0   At the traffic light, turn left onto US 1A, also called Sagamore Road, keeping the cemetery on your left. Continue on this road for 1.6 miles, passing the intersection where US 1B leads left toward New Castle, to a four-way intersection with a blinking light, where US 1A curves sharply left.

US 1A is a wide two-lane road through a residential section of Portsmouth. While there may be a substantial amount of traffic, the speed limit is low. You should ride as carefully here as you would in any city. Please note that the bridge just before the US 1B junction has open grates and should be walked over.

2.6   Where US 1A bears left towards Odiorne Point State Park (you will have a chance to explore the park and nature center on your return), you continue straight on Sagamore Road toward Rye Center.

The roads you cycle between this junction and Little Boars Head, where you pick up US 1A again, are narrow with fair surfaces, no shoulders, good visibility, and little traffic. The terrain is generally level.

Foyes Corner Market, a well stocked group store located at the junction of Sagamore Road and US 1A, is open all day every day.

3.6   Where Clark Road forks straight, curve right to stay on Sagamore Road.

4.1   At the next curve, bear right again on the road posted for Boston and Rye Center.

5.2   Just before you enter the center of Rye, your route merges with Washington Road. Bear right, on Washington Road, and pass the Rye School.

There is a Cumberland Farms grocery on the right where you join Washington Road.

5.6   In Rye Center, keep to the right of the war monument, following Washington Road toward Route 1, Boston, and Manchester.

Time seems to have stood still in this part of Rye. Salt marshes, woods, and gardens stretch away from the many huge old homes that line the road you follow. In the center of the village you can visit the burial ground from the Indian Massacre of 1691.

7.7   At the traffic light at the US 1 intersection, continue straight, following the road 1.7 miles to a stop sign just beyond the I-95 overpass.

At 7 miles on the corner of West Road and Sagamore stands the Hitching Post Country Store with crafts and collectibles (10–5 Mon.–Sat., noon–5 Sun.) and the Butt'ry Tea Room (10–5 Tues.–Sat., Sunday brunch 11–3, 964-8988).

9.4   At the stop sign, turn left onto NH 151 and cycle roughly parallel to the interstate for 2.5 miles, this time passing over the superhighway.

11.9   Just beyond the overpass, turn left onto the road marked for the Sagamore-Hampton Golf Course. Continue for 0.9 mile to a stop sign at the junction of US 1.

12.8   At the stop sign, turn left and then immediately right onto South Road. Cycle along this road 1.9 miles to Woodland Road.

14.7   At this corner, turn right onto Woodland Road and ride for 1.4 miles to the stop sign at the junction of US 101D (Atlantic Avenue).

16.1   At the junction, turn left and head toward Little Board Head, 1.2 miles away.

17.3   When you reach US 1A (Ocean Boulevard) at Little Boars Head, turn left for the 9.6 mile-ride along the seashore.

Along US 1A, you pass numerous seaside mansions with sweeping lawns and rose gardens and many smaller weathered structures with antique and craft shops. Rye Harbor State Park, a wayside park on a point of land jutting into the ocean and an ideal spot for a picnic, is located 4 miles beyond Little Boars Head. Wallis Sands State Park, 2.2 miles beyond Rye Harbor, is a well-known swimming and sunning spot, while Odiorne Point State Park, 1.6 miles north of Wallis Sands, offers picnicking and hiking trails. It is also the site of Fort Dearborn and an Audubon Center.

Along US 1A, there are numerous restaurants specializing in seafood and snacks. You can buy groceries all day every day at the Sandpiper Country Store and Coffee Shop adjacent to the Dunes Motel, 2.4 miles from Little Boars Head and at Philbrick's Store, 0.2 mile further on.

U.S. 1A along the Atlantic shoreline is narrow and winding with intermittent shoulder. There are also occasional paved walkways and a 0.9 mile bikepath through Odiorne Point State Park. However, you

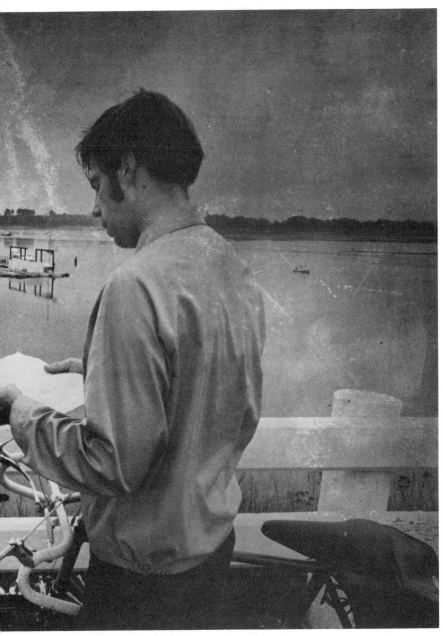

You should walk across the open-grate bridge by Wentworth-by-the-Sea, but the view of Little Harbor and Odiorne Point more than compensates for any inconvenience.

will have to share the roadway with cars for much of this stretch and traffic can be heavy, especially on summer weekends; so use extreme caution if you cycle then.

26.9   When you reach the blinking light at the four-way intersection (through which you continued straight on your way to Rye Center), turn right to retrace your way on US 1A for 0.5 mile, as far as the US 1B cutoff to New Castle.

27.4   At the junction, turn right onto US 1B and follow this route 4.2 miles through New Castle back to Portsmouth.

On US 1B you pass Wentworth-by-the-Sea, recently closed, but a reminder of the grandeur of late nineteenth century hotels. The town of New Castle, an island village dating back to 1623, is worth exploring. Its winding, narrow streets, Great Island Common, and the ruins of Fort Constitution combine to provide constant interest.

US 1B is, like US 1A, narrow and winding, but it carries less traffic. Exercise caution at the cross-grid bridge just before Wentworth-by-the-Sea and at the two bridges that bring you from Newcastle to Portsmouth. These last two have paved roadways but open-grate shoulders.

31.6   When you come again to the four-way intersection in Portsmouth by the Blue Fin fish market, turn right to retrace your route up Marcy Street to your start.

32.0   You are back at Prescott Park, where you began the tour.

Bicycle Repair Services

Gallager's Sport Center, Inc., Isling St., Portsmouth (436-7070).
Peddler's Bicycle Shop, 1 Cate St., Portsmouth (436-0660).

19
Litchfield-Londonderry

17.5 miles; easy to moderate

A green oasis surrounded by the state's major population centers, our Litch-field–Londonderry tour offers easy to moderate cycling, low traffic, and quick, easy access for most people in southern New Hampshire. Litchfield, a small community on the eastern bank of the Merrimack River, features basically level cycling and a nice warmup for later portions of the tour. Old farms with farm stands sell fresh vegetables and produce in season. Orchards invite the ambitious to "pick your own." The more heavily wooded town of Londonderry is hillier with frequent but gentle undulations that contrast nicely with the open farms and flood plains of Litchfield. Londonderry was settled in 1718 by Scotch emigrants who came here via the northern Ireland city of Londonderry after which the NH town was named. Pockets of suburban development note the presence of population growth in southern New Hampshire but do not seriously detract from the quality of the experience. The town center with churches, grange and green are a pleasant reminder of bygone days.

To get to your starting point, take the Everett Turnpike to exit 5 in Nashua. Follow NH 111 (Hollis Street) east for 2.7 miles to NH 3A just across the Merrimack in Hudson. Follow NH 3A north for 5.4 miles to its junction with Pinecrest Road. From Manchester, follow NH 3A (Brown Avenue) south from its junction with I-293 for 9 miles to the junction of Pinecrest Road.

0.0 Head north on NH 3A for 4.6 miles to its junction with Corning Road.

NH 3A is a level, two-lane road with a double yellow centerline and no shoulder. Because it connects Hudson and Manchester, traffic can be moderate to heavy during commuter hours. It is flat and reasonably straight, thereby affording reasonably good visibility for both cyclist and driver.

At 0.6 mile, you will find The Old Litchfield Tavern Gift Shop (10–10 Thurs.–Sat., 1–5 Sun.), a nicely maintained old colonial with a large barn. The Litchfield Town Hall, Fire Department, and white frame Presbyterian Church (founded 1809) are located just beyond the gift shop.

McQuesten, Nanticook, and Durocher North farm stands are located on the left at 1.6, 1.8, and 3.1 miles respectively. They are open only during the summer and early fall.

Terra Nova Restaurant, located at 3.3 miles, offers a lounge and fine Italian dining (lunch 11:30–2:30 Tues.–Sat.; dinner at 5, 3:30 Sun.;

closed Mon.; 424-6546 for reservations). Ma's Country Kitchen, at 3.6 miles, offers home cooked food with daily specials, grinders and piz- zas (2:30–10 Mon.–Fri., 10–10 Sat. and Sun.). Pantry Pride Con- venience Mart is located adjacent to Ma's Country Kitchen (open all day, every day).

4.6   Turn right on Corning Road, which later becomes Litchfield Road, and ride 3.5 miles to its junction with NH 128. Note that Corning Road is located across the street from Dar-Col Stable which offers riding lessons (424-3150).

Corning Road initially is a wide, flat, smoothly paved road which im- mediately goes through a small residential area. After 0.4 mile, the road becomes narrower and the surroundings more rural. At 0.6 mile, the road begins to ascend away from the Merrimack River. The road curves and rises, with occasional short descents, through old New England countryside to NH 128. The ascents, though frequent, are gentle and short, and should present little difficulty.

There are no services on this road.

8.1   Ride across NH 128 and immediately bear right at a fork in the road onto

An early spring ride along a swollen river.

Stonehenge Road. (Do not bear left onto Bartley Hill Road.) From NH 128 ride 0.7 mile to the junction of Hardy Road on the right. Turn right on Hardy Road and continue for 1.8 miles to a stop sign and the junction with Pillsbury Road. Turn right on Pillsbury and proceed for 1 mile to its junction with NH 128 in Londonderry.

Stonehenge Road immediately begins a moderate ascent, passing through a residential area, and soon becomes rural once again. It is a typical New Hampshire backroad: narrow, no shoulder or centerline and light traffic.

Hardy Road is another typical narrow backroad with no shoulder or centerline. But the stonewalls and trees that line the road make it a pleasant ride. You climb gradually for 0.7 mile to the entrance to Birchwood Ski Area and then level out and descend all the way to Pillsbury Road. Beyond the ski area, the land becomes more suburban as you approach Londonderry. Pillsbury Road, wider and smoother than Hardy Road, ascends gradually for 0.7 mile before a short descent to the junction of NH 128.

There are no services on this section of the tour.

11.6   Ride across NH 128 and continue on Pillsbury Road for 1.3 miles to its junc-

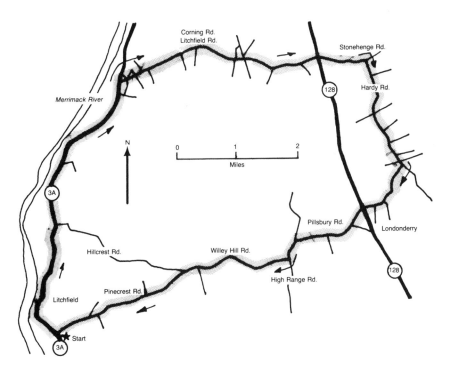

tion with High Range Road. Turn left on High Range road and ride 0.3 mile to the junction on the right of Willey Hill Road. Turn right on Willey Hill Road and ride 1.9 miles to a fork in the road and the junction of Hillcrest Road and Pinecrest Road. Bear left on Pinecrest road and ride 1.4 miles to its junction with NH 3A.

At the junction of Pillsbury Road and NH 128, the Londonderry Grange #44, Londonderry Presbyterian Church (constructed 1837), United Methodist Church and a town green, complete with war monument and bandstand, offer a pleasant and refreshing look at old new England.

A short descent down Pillsbury Road from its junction with NH 128 will bring you to Mack's Apple Orchard where you can pick your own in season.

Pillsbury, High Range and Pinecrest Roads generally have the usual backroad characteristics with no shoulder, or centerline, some frost heaves and generally low traffic. While there are a few short ascents, the descents are longer and more frequent as you head towards the Merrimack River and your starting point. Mostly rural in nature with trees frequently forming a shaded tunnel over the road, this last section offers a pleasant end to your tour.

There are no services on this section of the tour.

17.5 Arrive back at your starting point at the junction of Pinecrest Road and NH 3A.

Bicycle Repair Services

There are no bicycle shops on this route, however Manchester to the north and Hudson to the south both have repair services.

The Bike Barn, 255 Maple St., Manchester (668-6555).

Hetzer's Bicycle Shop, 5 Lowell Rd., Hudson (882-5566).

Jake's Bicycle Shop, 414 Kelley St., Manchester (669-5422).

A.T. Nault and Son, 32 Bridge St., Manchester (669-7993).

Lakes Region

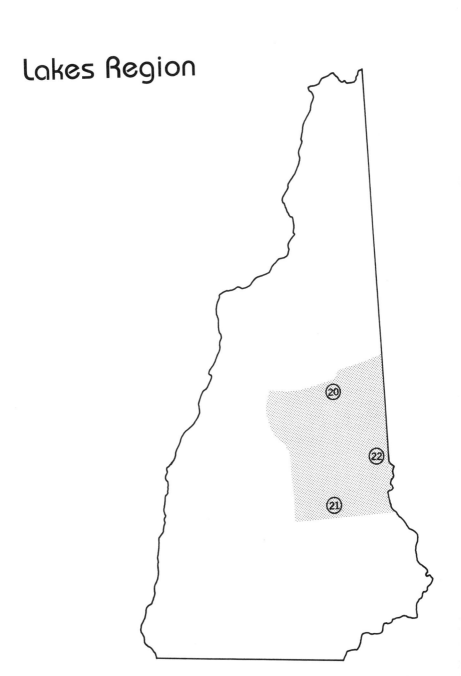

114

20
Tamworth-North Sandwich

23.1 miles; moderate cycling
Rolling to hilly terrain, some short steep hills

Between the White Mountain National Forest in the north and Lake Winnipesaukee in the south, this area is surprisingly free of commercial recreational services and development. For the cyclist, this is a rather happy circumstance. Not unlike a quiet child who is often overshadowed by the obvious exploits of an older sibling, it is a section of New Hampshire whose charm and beauty becomes apparent only upon close examination. Let the masses hike the mountains and swim in the lakes; leave the little country roads in Tamworth, Wonalancet, and North Sandwich the domain of the cyclist.

Passing through a mixture of farms, forests, and one-store towns, this is a good trip for someone who seeks a respite from the rush of urban life or the pressures of a demanding job. Because the area is not overrun with numerous activities to entice you off your bike, you should be content to negotiate the twists and turns and ups and downs of backcountry roads. And while the tour covers enough distance and hills to make you know you have been cycling, it is also a trip that should not leave you exhausted and spent.

Two country inns are located near the starting point of your trip. In Chocorua, exactly 2 miles east of the NH 113 and NH 113A junction, is Stafford's in the Field (323-7766), a thirteen-room inn set on a knoll and surrounded by acres of rolling fields. It offers a quiet, relaxed setting and serves breakfast and dinner daily. The Tamworth Inn (323-7721) on the Main Street of Tamworth, where you start this tour, is a 22-room, 1800s village inn. In addition to lodging, it serves dinner nightly 6–8:30 and Sunday brunch 11–2. The tavern is open until 1 AM and there is usually live entertainment on weekends.

Your tour begins on the main street of Tamworth, near the junction of NH 113 and NH 113A. You should have no problem finding parking.

0.0 From the center of Tamworth, cycle back to the junction of NH 113 and NH 113A.

The Barnstormers Playhouse, located at the west end of Tamworth's main street, houses a summer theater group that is the oldest in New Hampshire and one of the oldest in the United States. It was founded by Francis Grover Cleveland, son of our twenty-second president, in 1931. While the players once did an eighty-mile circuit, they now perform only at their Tamworth home.

Remick's Country Store (8–7 Mon.–Sat., 8–3 Sun.) in Tamworth has a small deli and is the only place to buy food until you reach North Sandwich, approximately fourteen miles into your trip.

0.1   At the junction of numbered highways, turn left onto NH 113A, heading towards Wonalancet.

NH 113A, the Chinook Trail, is a very windy, roller-coaster road with a rough surface and no shoulder. Visibility is generally poor due to frequent dips and curves, but because traffic tends to be light, this should not present a major problem.

1.1   When the road forks, stay left and head up a short hill. This fork is well marked with signs for Wonalancet, Sandwich, and NH 113A, all pointing in the direction you are going. Continue on this winding road for 5.6 miles to Wonalancet.

Big Pines Natural Area, part of Hemenway State Forest, is located on the left, 1.8 miles north of the fork. Its cool, shady woods are inviting on a hot day.

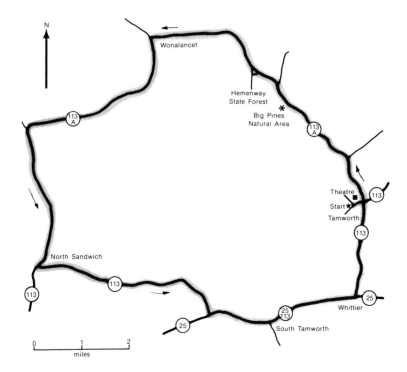

6.7   In Wonalancet, NH 113A turns sharply left. Turn left and follow it for 6.9
miles to NH 113 in North Sandwich.

    The countryside is very pleasant with rolling farmland, stone fences,
and stands of birch and pine through which you get occasional glimpses
of the nearby mountains.

    This stretch of NH 113A is similar to the one you just traveled: traffic
is light, but visibility is poor and there is no shoulder.

13.6   In North Sandwich, turn left onto NH 113 and ride for 3.9 miles to the junction with NH 25.

    In North Sandwich food supplies are available at Old North Sandwich
Store (8–7 Mon.–Sat., 9–5 Sun.); instead of turning left at the junction
of NH 113A and NH 113, continue straight for 0.2 mile to the village
proper. The store, which has a very good deli, is on the right.

    Road conditions on NH 113 are similar to those on NH 113A.

17.5   At the intersection with NH 25, turn left onto NH 25/NH 113 and ride for
3.2 miles along the Bearcamp River through South Tamworth to Whittier.
The numbered highways split in Whittier just beyond the Whittier Cash
Market.

    The Country Store (open all day, every day), a small grocery, is locat-

Mountain vistas are just some of the many treats on the Tamworth-North Sandwich tour.

ed on the left at 18.4 miles. Food can be purchased at the Whittier Cash Market (7–7 daily). Adjacent to the Whittier Cash Market is the Pioneer Restaurant and Snack Bar.

NH 25 is a primary New Hampshire route. This section has a smooth surface and a fairly consistent three-foot-wide paved shoulder that occasionally disappears when the road crosses a narrow bridge. Traffic tends to be moderate and steady. Because it is quite level, offers good visibility, and has a ridable shoulder, it is a reasonably safe road to cycle, despite the traffic.

20.7 At the fork in Whittier, bear left onto NH 113 and proceed for 2.3 miles back to the road to Tamworth village.

Chequers Villa, an Italian American Restaurant and Lounge is located on NH 113 0.5 mile north of the intersection where NH 25 and NH 113 divide.

23.0 At the junction of NH 113 and NH 113A, turn left onto the main street of Tamworth.

23.1 You are back at your start.

Bicycle Repair Services

The nearest bicycle shops are located in North Conway. Please refer to Tour #18.

21

Gilmanton Triangle

15.4 miles, moderate to difficult
Hilly terrain

Gilmanton Corner, Gilmanton Ironworks and Lower Gilmanton form a little triangle on the hilly western edge of New Hampshire Lakes Region. Originally named Gilmanton after a large family, The Gilmans, many of who received grants from Lieutenant-Governor John Wentworth of Massachusetts during his brief jurisdiction over New Hampshire, it was once much larger and one of the most populous towns in the state. Now it is a quiet community removed from the more intense activity around Lakes Winnipesaukee, Winnisquam and Squam. The three tiny villages with their rural ambiance, provide a beautiful setting for a short but hilly trip.

For those who wish to lengthen their exploration of the Lakes Region, it is easy to connect this tour with the Wolfeboro–Ossipee Tour. Simply follow NH 140 northeast out of Gilmanton Ironworks, named for an ill-fated underwater iron mining operation, for six miles to Alton and then take NH 28 north into Alton Bay where you catch the M/S Mount Washington across Lake Winnipesaukee to Wolfeboro on Tuesday, Thursday, Saturday and Sunday at 10:15 AM from Memorial Day to October 21 (also at 1:30 PM from June 5 to Labor Day). They take bicycles free of charge. Cost: $4.50/person (366-5531 or 4837).

In an attempt to minimize the ascents and maximize the descents on this trip we calculated the ups and downs in both directions and found it only slightly more advantageous to ride it in a counter clockwise direction. Total descents were only 0.5 mile longer than total ascents. Things do tend to balance out.

While there are no overnight accomodations within Gilmanton, many of the surrounding towns such as Pittsfield, Alton, Gilford and Laconia have motels and cottages. Oak Birch Inn on NH 28A in Alton Bay is a turn of the century inn with a panoramic view of Lake Winnipesaukee, private beach, dining room and tavern (875-5200).

Begin this tour at the junction of NH 107 and Old Stage Road in Lower Gilmanton, 0.7 mile north of the junction of NH 129 and NH 107. Park alongside Old Stage Road.

0.0   Follow Old Stage Road 4.3 miles to its junction with NH 140 in Gilmanton Ironworks.

Old Stage Road is a real New Hampshire backroad. There is no shoulder or center line, and the frost heaves will occasionally make you airborne if you're not careful to ride around them. However, it offers some good views and about 3.6 miles of level and descending (sometimes steeply) terrain. Do not take any turns off Old Stage Road as it twists and turns towards Gilmanton Ironworks. With the exception of White Oak Road on the right, 0.7 mile before Gilmanton Ironworks, any wrong turns you might make will quickly turn to dirt.

There are no facilities on this part of the tour.

4.3 In Gilmanton Ironworks turn left onto NH 140 and continue for 6.5 miles into Gilmanton, sometimes referred to as Gilmanton Corner.

The Village Store at the junction of Old Stage Road and NH 140 is a good place for lunch or a snack. Open 9–7 every day, it has daily specials and a deli for fresh sandwiches. Some of the specials include fish chowder, beef stew or chili ($1.25 per cup, $2.25 per bowl). Hamburgers and cheeseburgers are $1.25 and $1.50 respectively.

NH 140 is a wide road with a smooth surface and low to moderate traffic. It has a paved shoulder for a short distance as you enter Gilmanton. With gradual rises and dips all the way to Gilmanton, it is as enjoyable as a roller coaster ride. With the exception of one long ascent of 1.3 miles starting 2.4 miles from Gilmanton Ironworks, most of the ups and downs are 0.2 to 0.6 mile in length.

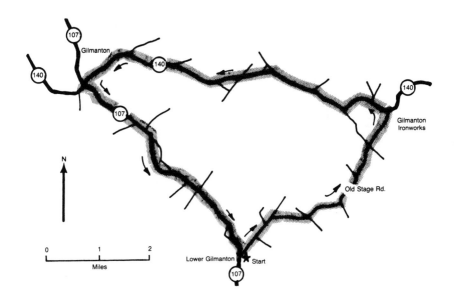

10.8   In Gilmanton turn left on NH 107 and ride 4.6 miles back to your starting
point at the junction of Old Stage Road and NH 107.

NH 107 is a two-lane road with smooth surface and no shoulder. Built
in 1770, it is one of the earliest highways in New Hampshire and served
as a supply route between the port of Durham and settlements in Coos
County. Today this beautiful country road offers exceptional views of
New Hampshire's Lakes Region. With the exception of one gradual
ascent of 0.4 mile and a steep ascent of 0.8 mile, the terrain will be
level to descending all the way back to Old Stage Road.

Big old homes with stone walls grace the main street of Gilmanton, as do the town library, Congregational Church, an old tavern (now
a private residence), and the Gilmanton Academy Building. Founded
in 1795 and graduating its last class in 1910, the academy was a highly regarded school which also had a theological seminary from 1846

A quiet pastoral scene on the Gilmanton triangle tour.

until after the Civil War. Currently on the National Register of Historic Sites, it was used as the village school until the 1940s, and is now used for various town functions.

Gilmanton Corner Store, located at the junction of NH 140 and NH 107, (7:30–7 Mon.–Sat., 7:30–6 Sun.), is a good place to buy food for lunch or a snack and enjoy the atmosphere of this lovely New England setting.

15.4   Arrive back at the junction of NH 107 and Old Stage Road.

22

Wolfeboro-Ossipee

37.8 miles; moderate rolling terrain
Some moderate to steep hills

Wolfeboro, starting point for this trip, is located on the southeastern shore of Lake Winnipesaukee, New Hampshire's largest lake with 72 square miles of water surface, 283 miles of shoreline and 274 habitable islands. John Wentworth, last royal governor of New Hampshire, built a summer home on nearby Lake Wentworth in 1763 and as a result, the town became known as the "Oldest Summer Resort in America." Living up to its name, the town has a very attractive Main Street overlooking Wolfeboro Bay and is a center of activity for the region with a summer playhouse, golf course, many fine restaurants and numerous overnight accommodations. Attractions such as the Wolfeboro Railroad and the M/S Mount Washington Cruise Ship, which stops in Wolfeboro every day, also offer the opportunity for a non-cycling view of New Hampshire's Lakes Region. Brewster Academy, a private, co-ed boarding and day school for grades 9–12, overlooks the Bay from its attractive campus in town near the junction of NH 28 and NH 109.

For the cyclist this trip offers the option of either a moderate day tour or a weekend/mini vacation getaway. Once away from Wolfeboro you will quickly find yourself in rolling countryside with frequent views of the region's numerous lakes, nicely maintained old houses, farm stands, occasional craft and antique shops, and enough small towns with stores and restaurant to keep you adequately stocked with food and beverages. We did not recommend a loop along or around Lake Winnipesaukee due to the potential for heavy traffic conditions, especially on summer weekends, and the general lack of paved shoulder. The Nordic Skier Shop at the corner of Main and Mill Streets sells, rents and repairs bicycles (9:30–5:30 Mon.–Sat., 569-3151).

Ample lodging is available in and around Wolfeboro, however, make advanced reservations during the busy summer months. If you like the charm of old New England, consider the Wolfeboro Inn (569-3016) at the north end of town overlooking the lake. It offers bed and breakfast accommodations and has a restaurant and lounge as well.

Start at Wolfeboro Shopping Center on NH 109/NH 28, 0.2 mile from the junction of these two roads in Wolfeboro. Ample parking is available in this area.

0.0 From the Wolfeboro Shopping Center turn left heading northeast on NH

109/NH 28 through Wolfeboro and Wolfeboro Falls for 2.9 miles to Wolfe-boro Center where these two roads diverge.

NH 109/NH 28 is a two-lane road with a narrow paved shoulder vary-ing in width from one to two feet. Traffic will generally be light to moderate. The road rises gradually as you ride away from Lake Winni-pesaukee, and good views of Crescent Lake can be seen at 1.4 miles.

Stores and restaurants, too numerous to mention here, abound in Wolfeboro. A number of convenience stores, restaurants, and farm stands are available along the route to meet your needs for food and beverages.

2.9 Turn right on NH 109, heading towards Brookfield and Wakefield, and ride 9.1 miles to its junction with NH 16. Note that there is a fork in the road after 7.9 miles where NH 109 bears left and the Governor John Wentworth Highway bears right. Stay to the left on NH 109.

A very scenic road, NH 109 is level as it hugs the shore of Lake Went-worth for 2.5 miles and has been resurfaced for the first 2.2 miles. The surface for the remaining 6.9 miles is still good quality with very few frost heaves or pot holes. There is no shoulder but traffic is usually light.

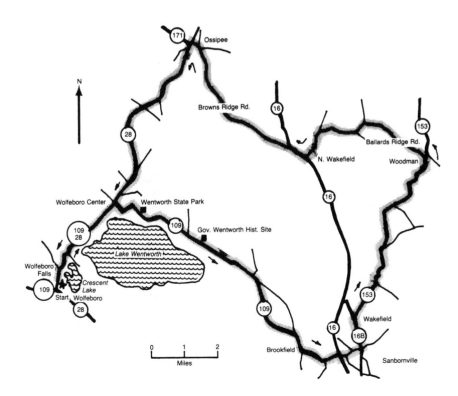

After a gradual climb of 1.1 miles, the road rises and falls, usually gently but occasionally steeply, for the next 5.5 miles. These ascents and descents vary from 0.1 to 0.5 mile in length.

Wentworth State Park, located adjacent to NH 109, 4.3 miles from your starting point, offers picnicking and swimming at Clow's Beach, a long sandy section of Lake Wentworth. The Governor John Wentworth Historic Site, at 5.7 miles, is the location of the country house of the last royal governor of New Hampshire which was built in 1763. It was this house that gave rise to the prominence of Wolfeboro as "The Oldest Summer Resort in America." The tall pines surrounding the site are a great place to picnic.

Fletcher Farm at 7.7 miles and Maynard's Farm Stand at 11.8 miles offer fresh fruits and vegetables in season.

12.0   Proceed across NH 16 and continue on NH 109 for 0.8 mile to its junction with NH 16B/NH 153. Turn left and ride 1.1 miles to where NH 16B and NH 153 split. Bear right and follow NH 153 for 5.1 miles to its junction with Ballards Ridge Road in Woodman.

Wolfeboro train station in downtown Wolfeboro is the starting point for a ride on the Wolfeboro Railroad.

NH 109 remains a two-lane road with no shoulder as it passes through a residential area and into the center of Sanbornville. NH 153 is a twisting, rolling road with good surface, no shoulder, low to moderate traffic and lots of pretty views as it winds past the numerous lakes and gentle hills of this area.

Sanbornville is the southeast terminus of the Wolfeboro Railroad, a tourist attraction which conducts rides between here and Wolfeboro daily from mid-May to mid-October (569-4884). There are several restaurants and food stores in town should you wish to take a lunch or snack break. Sarah's Spa Restaurant (open at 6 AM), Luv'n Oven Bakery and Richard's Market are located on NH 109 just beyond the railroad station and town hall. Poor Richard's Pub is located at the junction of NH 109 and NH 153/16B.

Lovell Brook Antiques (11–4:30 Sat.–Tues., and by appointment) specializing in old tools and furniture is located at the junction of NH 16 and NH 109. Westlock Yarn Craft (10–5 daily) is situated in Wakefield.

A and B Mini Market (8–after dark every day) and Seven Lakes Take Out are located on NH 153, 3.5 miles from Sanbornville.

19.0   Turn left on Ballards Ridge Road (located between two houses at the Woodman Town Line) and ride 4.6 miles to its junction with NH 16 in North Wakefield. Turn right on NH 16, continue for 0.5 mile to Browns Ridge Road on the left. Follow Browns Ridge Road for 4.6 miles to its junction with NH 171 in Ossipee.

Ballards Ridge Road is a typical New Hampshire back road, with frost heaves, no shoulder and no center line. After 0.3 mile, it begins a gradual rise for 0.5 mile and is steep for another 0.3 mile before leveling off

M/S *Mount Washington* plies the waters of Lake Winnepesaukee.

at Twin Cedar Farm Stand. Thereafter, it descends, except for one short steep ascent, for 3.5 miles to NH 16. NH 16 is a wide, level, two-lane road with paved shoulder that widens briefly to four lanes with shoulder near its junction with Browns Ridge Road. The condition of Browns Ridge Road is similar to Ballards Ridge Road. After 0.5 mile, you must climb a fairly steep hill for 0.5 mile. From this point the road has frequent, short ups and downs for 3.6 miles to Ossipee. Lined with trees that form a shady tunnel and well kept old homes with fine views and stone walls, Browns Ridge Road offers a pleasant ride.

Pine River Steak House (4–9 Wed. and Thurs., 4–10 Fri., 12–10 Sat., 12–9 Sun.) and Pine River Pond General Store, where you can buy food for a picnic (open daily) are located on Ballards Ridge Road 1.1 miles from its junction with NH 16. Moulton's Store (founded 1910) is located in Ossipee near the junction of NH 171 and Browns Ridge Road (open daily).

28.7 Bear left on NH 171 and ride down the picturesque main street of Ossipee past the Carroll County Courthouse and Second Congregational Church for 0.3 mile to the junction with NH 28. Turn left and continue for 8.8 miles back to Wolfeboro.

NH 28 is a two-lane road with a smooth, well graded surface, long gradual ascents and descents, and a paved shoulder that varies in width from a full lane down to one foot. Generally you will have an adequate shoulder to ride although it narrows significantly as you go through Wolfeboro Falls and Wolfeboro.

37.8 Arrive back at Wolfeboro Shopping Center. Note that this tour could be reduced by 5.8 miles by beginning at the junction of NH 28 and NH 109 in Wolfeboro Center or at Wentworth State Park. The starting point in Wolfeboro was selected so you could incorporate a ride through the town at the beginning or end of your tour.

North Country

23

North Conway-Bear Notch

38.7 miles; moderate to challenging cycling
Level to rolling terrain, many downgrades and one long, gradual climb

North Conway, the starting point for this trip, is a year-round resort community located on US 302/NH 16 at the southeastern edge of the White Mountain National Forest. As the major gateway to the Presidential Range, it offers a wide variety of services to the tourist and outdoor lover, including numerous specialty shops, restaurants, and overnight accommodations. Because thousands of people disperse from this town each year to the White Mountains, it is difficult to develop a trip here that avoids high traffic conditions at least part of the way. Coupled with the traffic problem is that of extremely long upgrades, which can make cycling a punishment rather than a pleasure, especially for the weekend cyclist. Nonetheless, our North Conway-Bear Notch trip offers an excellent opportunity to see by bicycle a particularly beautiful section of New Hampshire. The route we have chosen involves only one long, gradual climb, through Bear Notch. The rest of the way winds along the Saco and Swift rivers through level to rolling terrain and includes lots of gentle downgrades to make cycling exhilerating and effortless. To put the icing on the cake, the road conditions are quite good, the traffic generally light, and the scenery spectacular.

There is plenty of lodging in the Mount Washington Valley area all the way from Conway to Jackson. This region attracts tourists especially in the summer and during foliage season. To insure suitable accommodations, we suggest that you take advantage of the free information and reservation service offered by the Mount Washington Valley Chamber of Commerce, Box 385, North Conway, NH 03860. Simply call 356-3171 or stop by the booth on Main Street in the center of North Conway. During off-season, hours are 10–4. During peak season, hours are longer, generally extending into the evening.

If you like little inns and guest houses, like we do, here are a few suggestions. Wild Flowers Guest House (356-2224), located on NH 16, 1.5 miles north of North Conway Village, is a charming 1879 house complete with a woodstove in the parlor and fireplace in the breakfast nook. We also recommend Sunny Side Lodge (356-6239) on Seavey Street, a short walk or ride from downtown. Finally, the Center Chimney (356-6788) and the Nereledge Inn (356-2831) are both on River Road within walking distance of town and on the route of your tour.

There are lots of good places to eat as well. Horsefeathers (11:30–midnight daily) on Main Street (NH16) is a very popular pub/restaurant with great food. Around the corner on Seavey Street is Montana's (11:30–11:30/daily), a similar type of place. For full course dinners, the Red Parka Pub (5–10 daily) at the junction of NH 16 and US 302 in Glen and the Oxen Yoke (5:30 on plus Sunday Brunch) are good choices.

Your route begins at the north end of North Conway, near the Eastern Mountain Sports shop and the Eastern Slopes Inn, where there is unmetered on-street parking.

0.0 Head north on US 302/NH 16 a very short distance to River Road, on the left by the Gulf station and just beyond the Eastern Mountain Sports store.

US 302/NH 16 within North Conway is a busy road where traffic is often heavy but slow moving.

0.1 At the intersection, turn left onto River Road, riding downhill under the railroad bridge toward the Saco River, which you cross in 1 mile.

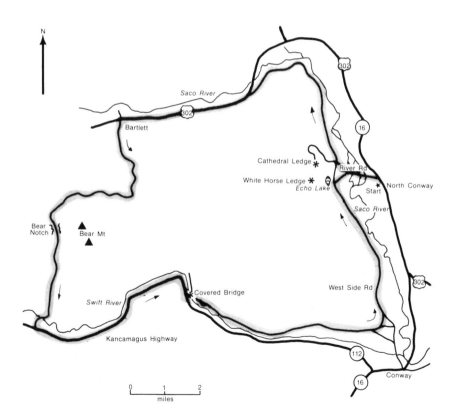

River Road tends to be narrow with no shoulder.

Just under the railroad bridge at 0.2 mile are the Nereledge Inn and Center Chimney Guest House mentioned earlier.

1.1   Immediately after crossing the Saco River, your road merges with West Side Road, which comes in from the left. Continue straight on this road for another 5.6 miles to US 302.

At the junction with West Side Road you can see clearly White Horse and Cathedral ledgers, two rock cliffs rising abruptly from the valley floor. In 0.5 mile you pass a paved access road to Cathedral Ledge; the climb to the top is tough for cyclists, but the view from there is outstanding. Foot trails also provide an easy hike to the top. Diana's Baths, a popular natural area with smooth rocks and refreshing pools, can be reached by trail from West Side Road approximately 1 mile beyond the turnoff for Cathedral Ledge. A historical marker commemorating Ladey Blance, a noted writer and contributor to *Harpers* and the *Atlantic Monthly* who lived in a nearby cottage, is located on the right 0.7 mile beyond the trail to Diana's Bath.

This stretch of road also tends to be narrow with no shoulder. The visibility is generally good although there are sections where the road curves and rolls enough to restrict your vision. Traffic patterns are difficult to predict in this area, but this road is certainly less traveled than US 302/NH 16.

6.7   At the intersection with US 302, turn left and ride for 4.1 miles to the blinking light in Bartlett just beyond the Bartlett Hotel.

W.W. Doolittle's Restaurant and Lounge (11:30–9:30) is located at Attitash Mountain Village (7.8 miles).

There are several restaurants and a few food stores along the section of US 302 you travel and in the village of Bartlett.

US 302 is a wide, two-lane road with a smooth surface, and intermittent shoulder, and excellent visibility. It is one of the three major roads through the White Mountains, so there is moderate to heavy traffic traveling at highway speeds. Because of its width and good visibility it can be ridden safely by the competent cyclist. Caution is urged, however.

10.8 From the blinking light in Bartlett, turn left onto Bear Notch Road.

Bartlett Village Store (open all day, every day) is at the junction of US 302 and Bear Notch Road. It sells coffee, donuts and subs as well as basic groceries.

There are several turnoffs along Bear Notch Road that offer excellent views of the Presidential Range.

Bear Notch Road is a forest highway with light traffic. It is wide, has good visibility, and has been nicely graded to provide a smooth, gradual rise over the 4.1-mile ascent to Bear Notch. Once over the crest, you have a 4.4-mile downgrade to NH 112, the Kancamagus Highway.

19.3   At the intersection, turn left onto the Kancamagus Highway, and ride 6.1
miles to the covered bridge at Blackberry Crossing.

Be sure to stop at the Rocky Gorge Scenic Area, on the left, 3.5 miles
beyond the junction of Bear Notch Road, and at Lower Falls Scenic
Area, also on the left 2 miles beyond Rocky Gorge. Both offer opportunities to swim in the clear, rushing waters of the Swift River and to
picnic by the waterfalls.

The Kancamagus Highway has an even better surface than Bear
Notch Road but carries much more traffic, especially on weekends.
Although visibility is excellent and traffic tends to travel at low speeds,
we urge you to use caution here.

The Albany Bridge leads you off the Kancamagus Highway onto a lightly traveled
back road.

25.4 At Blackberry Crossing, turn left onto Dugway Road and immediately cross the Swift River through a covered bridge. Take an immediate right on the far side of the bridge and ride for 6.6 miles to West Side Road; there is no sign posted here.

The Albany covered bridge was built in 1859.

From Blackberry Crossing to West Side Road, the road is a narrow, country byway with some frost heaves, no shoulder, and lots of dips, rises, and curves. While visibility is restricted and road conditions are poor, traffic tends to be very light.

32.0 At the junction by West Side Road, turn left and cycle 5.6 miles back to River Road by the Saco River.

About .5 mile before you reach River Road you pass Echo Lake State Park, which offers picnicking, hiking and swimming.

West Side Road is quite level and provides for easy cycling. It is smooth but lacks a shoulder. Traffic is usually light to moderate.

37.6 At the junction with River Road, turn right and cycle back to US 302/NH 16 and your car.

38.7 You are back at your start by the Eastern Mountain Sports store in North Conway.

Bicycle Repair Services

The Bike Shop, Mountain Valley Mall, North Conway (356-6089).

Joe Jones Bike Specialists, Main St., North Conway (356-2891).

The Sports Outlet, Route 16, North Conway (356-3133).

24
Sugar Hill

14.4 miles; moderate cycling
Level to rolling terrain, one long hill

Sugar Hill is a small, "undeveloped" resort town on the western slope of the White Mountains. Commanding exceptional views of the surrounding countryside, its name comes from a large grove of sugar maples found in the area. Having broken ties with the adjacent town of Lisbon in 1962, it is New Hampshire's youngest town.

We selected Sugar Hill as the focal point of this short trip because it couples scenic beauty with low traffic conditions and avoids the commercial development that characterizes many other tourist "meccas" in the White Mountains. Although you can easily complete the loop in a morning or afternoon, if you bring a picnic lunch and the weather invites swimming it can also be easily stretched out to a leisurely all-day affair. From a lazy cyclist's point of view, the only drawback is the long (nearly five miles) gradual climb to Sugar Hill, but that comes in the middle part of the tour after you have warmed up your cycling muscles. It also means that you can cap the tour with an equally long descent.

We suggest you start this trip in Lisbon, midway between the towns of Woodsville and Littleton on US 302/NH 10. Parking is available in and around the center of town.

While there is no lodging available in Lisbon, there are several inns in Sugar Hill, the midway point on your trip. An alternative is to start this tour in Sugar Hill and brave the long climb at the end of the day. Southworth's Bed and Breakfast (823-5344), located on NH 117, 0.2 mile east of its junction with Pearl Lake Road and directly across the street from the Sugar Hill Meeting House, offers cozy accommodations. The Homestead (823-5564 or 9577), located another 0.9 mile beyond Southworth's, has seventeen rooms in two buildings, including seven with private bath, and serves breakfast and dinner daily. With commanding views of the White Mountains, its porch is indeed inviting after a day of cycling. Many travelers have enjoyed this inn over its 100-year history. If you turn right at the Homestead and ride another 0.4 mile, you will come to Sunset Hill House (823-5522), a 35-room inn that features equally spectacular views of the Franconia Range. Offering three meals a day in five dining rooms, a bar, lounge, swimming pool with separate whirlpool and nine-hole golf course, it has just about every modern convenience.

Stands of birch line Pearl Lake Road, your return route on the Sugar Hill tour.

0.0   From the junction of US 302/NH 10 and School Street (unmarked but directly across the street from Northrop's IGA) in the center of town, head west on School Street, immediately crossing the Ammonoosuc River. Just beyond the bridge, by the Lisbon Town Hall, a large red Victorian frame structure, turn right onto Water Street/Lyman Road.

For more than three miles you parallel the Ammonoosuc River, which meanders through a narrow valley dotted with farm buildings and open fields.

The only place to buy food on this trip is Northrop's IGA supermarket (7–9 Mon–Sat., 9–6 Sun.) on NH 10 in the middle of Lisbon, directly across the street from your starting point. It is well stocked but has no deli. The only restaurant is Chevalos Pizza Plus located several doors north from Northrop's IGA (open all day Mon.–Sat., but closed on Sunday).

The roads paralleling the Ammonoosuc are narrow with fairly rough but ridable surfaces over level to rolling terrain. While there is no shoulder, the traffic is very light.

0.8   Just beyond the New Hampshire Electrical Cooperative building, on the right, turn right onto an unmarked road and continue along the Ammonoosuc River for another 2 miles to a junction with another unmarked road.

2.8   At the junction, turn right onto the unmarked road and ride 0.5 mile to US 302/NH 10.

3.3   At the junction, turn right onto the numbered highway, cross another bridge over the Ammonoosuc, and immediately turn left onto NH 117. You cycle

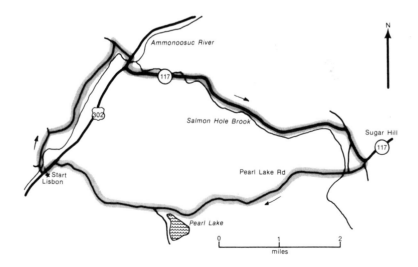

up this road for 4.9 miles to reach the village of Sugar Hill.

NH 117 follows Salmon Hole Brook, reputed at one time to have an inexhaustable supply of fish. Whether that reputation holds true today is doubtful, but fishless or not, the brook does offer occasional opportunities to cool off on a hot summer day.

NH 117 is wider than the roads you have just traveled and has a smooth surface. Its shoulder is of variable quality, however, and because it slopes away from the road it is not particularly enjoyable to ride. It does provide a place to pull off if necessary, though. While you are climbing steadily towards Sugar Hill on this stretch, road visibility and views of the surrounding countryside are excellent. Traffic tends to be light.

8.2 At the wood sign with white letters saying "Pearl Lake Road," turn sharply right and immediately begin a 6-mile-long descent back to Lisbon. After 0.2 mile there is a fork in the road. Stay to the right here.

At this junction, NH 117 curves upward and to the left into the village of Sugar Hill. If you can handle one more short ascent, follow it past the Pearl Lake Road turnoff through the center of the village and then turn around. You pass many pleasant homes as well as the Sugar Hill Meeting House on the left, a structure built in 1830 and capped with a cupola and clock. The village also offers some spectacular views of the surrounding countryside, with the White Mountains as a backdrop.

Pearl Lake Road offers an exceptionally scenic ride past open fields, farms, alongside a stream and through stands of pine and birch. Pearl Lake, on your left, is a gem with no development around it and no apparent restrictions on swimming.

Pearl Lake Road is narrow and bumpy with no shoulder, little traffic, some steep downgrades, and occasional sharp curves. Exercise caution on the downgrades, as it is easy here to get going too fast to negotiate some of the sharp curves safely.

14.2 At the fork 6 miles from Sugar Hill, bear right down a short steep hill and cross the railroad tracks to reach US 302/NH 10. Turn left and ride for 0.2 mile to your start.

US 302/NH 10 is a primary road with a smooth surface, moderate to heavy traffic, and very little shoulder. However, since you are within the Lisbon town limits, traffic tends to be slow for the short distance you must be on it.

14.4 You are back at your start by School Street.

Bicycle Repair Services

Littleton Bicycle Shop in Littleton is the nearest shop for this tour (444-3437).

25

Dixville Notch Century

105.7 miles; very challenging cycling (one-day tour) or moderate to challenging (two- or three-day tour) cycling
Level to rolling terrain, one long climb; then rolling to hilly terrain

A book on cycle touring would not be complete without a "Century ride" allowing the adventurous and experienced rider the opportunity to cover a hundred or more miles in one day. While New Hampshire's topographical extremes can make a Century a difficult goal to obtain, even for the experienced cyclist, our Dixville Notch trip offers a superb challenge to a wide segment of the cycling population, because those who aren't up to Century standards can easily convert this trip into a two- or three-day mini-vacation using either campsites or motels along the way.

With a mountain to cross and a number of hills to climb, especially in the trip's second half, the difficulty of this tour should not be underestimated. Much of the terrain, however, is level to gently rolling through some of the most beautiful and remote sections of New Hampshire. If you elect to take it you should be well equipped, have reasonable knowledge of bike maintenance, and carry a good tool kit, some spare parts, and emergency provisions in case you get stuck for the night.

This is not a trip that offers numerous alternate activities to complement your day of riding. You should love to ride and you should be able to appreciate the wonders of northern New Hampshire's wilderness: the Androscoggin River, Dixville Notch with its sheer cliffs edged by pines and white birches, and the Connecticut River while it is still a narrow, meandering stream. Probably one of the most appealing aspects of the trip is the openness of the terrain. Often in New Hampshire your view is restricted by heavy growth near the roadway; our Dixville Notch trip, however, tends to provide long, sweeping views of the north country.

The Traveler Motel (752-2500), 25 Pleasant St. (NH 16 south) at the south end of town, is one of the few places to stay in Berlin. Other motels, inns and campgrounds are mentioned as they occur along the route.

Begin your trip at the municipal parking lot on Mason St. (unmarked) near the City Hall in Berlin. To get there, take NH 16 North, passing the Berlin City Bank on your left, to the traffic light by City Hall and a Cumberland Farm Store (6–midnight daily), to your right. Turn right at this light and go over a bridge. Before you reach a second bridge, you come to a free municipal parking lot. If you plan to make this more than a one-day trip, we suggest you notify the Berlin Police that you are leaving your car overnight.

0.0   From the parking lot, retrace your route to NH 16 by City Hall, turn right onto NH 16 and ride for 1.7 miles to a traffic light just beyond Rotary Park.

There are numerous food stores and restaurants in Berlin and we strongly urge you to stock up before you leave town. Once you are north of this city, there is only one store until Errol. Berlin Foodliner, located on Pleasant Street adjacent to the Traveler Motel, is a large IGA with a good deli open every day 8:00 AM. Andy's Market, 0.5 mile north of your starting point, has a deli and is also open every day from 8:00 AM until early evening except Sunday when it closes at 2:00 PM. There are several other variety stores between here and your turnoff near Rotary Park.

NH 16 from City Hall to the traffic light by Rotary Park offers poor riding conditions through heavy traffic.

1.7   At the light, turn right, crossing a new steel bridge, and immediately bear left, heading north along the east bank of the Androscoggin River for 6.7 miles to Milan.

Although the Dixville Notch tour can be ridden as a Century, it passes through some lovely camping countryside.

The road on this side of the river is generally level with a smooth surface, little traffic and fair visibility. There is a good shoulder for the first 1.7 miles, but after that it disappears.

8.4   By the sign for NH 16 in Milan, adjacent to the Berlin Municipal Airport, turn left and cycle 0.4 mile, crossing the Androscoggin again, to NH 16. As soon as you cross the river at the junction of NH 16, you will find Young's Luncheonette and Variety Store, open all day, every day.

8.8   At the junction with NH 16, turn right. You cycle north on NH 16 for 21.6 miles to Errol.

While this entire section of the trip is wild and beautiful, Thirteen Mile Woods Scenic Area is particularly outstanding. Managed by the Seven Islands Land Company, the Brown Company, and the State of New Hampshire, there is no development of any kind along this stretch of road, which closely parallels the west bank of the Androscoggin and offers many places to stop and enjoy the solitude of wilderness. The

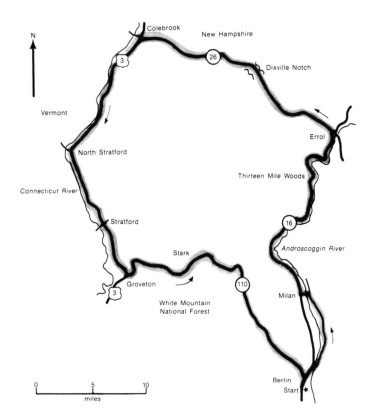

Androscoggin State Wayside Area 16.8 miles north of Milan has picnic tables and basic toilet facilities. The Androscoggin itself is a well-
known and very popular river for canoeing.

Camping is allowed by permit only along this section and only in
one designated area, Mollidgewock Campground, 19.2 miles north of
Milan. For information about the campground and permits, call
482-3373.

Saco Bound, Box 113, Center Conway, NH 03813, a canoe out-
fitting company, operates a whitewater school on the Androscoggin.
For information call 447-2177 or 3002.

From Milan to Errol, NH 16 has a smooth surface, little or no shoulder, excellent visibility, and, normally, light traffic. The terrain here is
flat to gently rolling.

30.4   In Errol, turn left onto NH 26 for the 22.3-mile ride through Dixville Notch
to the junction of US 3 in Colebrook.

With birch and fir trees growing out of sheer rock walls, Dixville Notch
makes this climb worth the effort, especially after you cross the top.
You are immediately rewarded with a view of the Balsams, a luxury
resort often referred to as America's Switzerland because of its setting,
architecture, and atmosphere.

Accommodations along this stretch of the route are available at
the Errol Motel (482-3256) located on NH 26, 0.3 mile east of its junction with NH 16; Log Haven Cabins and Camping Area (482-3294 or
3381), 7 miles west of Errol on NH 26; the Balsams Grand Resort Hotel
(225-3400), 4 miles further on; and at the Redwood Motel (237-8781)
6 miles east of Colebrook.

Food is available at Food Trade at the junction of NH 16 and NH
26 and at the Errol General Store and Post Office, located on NH 26,
0.2 mile east of its junction with NH 16. The Errol Restaurant, next door
to Food Trade, is open 4:30 AM–9 PM daily. Redwood Restaurant and
Country Store (part of the Redwood Motel) is open 7–10 daily. Sicard's
Bakery, open 7 days a week, is located 14.8 miles west of Errol, 500′
up the road to Coleman State Park.

NH 26 is a wide road with a smooth surface, good visibility, little
traffic, and generally very little shoulder. However, because it is a
primary highway, traffic tends to move fast. The terrain here is generally level to rolling through forest and farm country; the only significant
climb is 1.7 miles long up to Dixville Notch. West of the notch there
is a long, sinuous downgrade.

Dixville Notch is also on the political road map. During each
presidential election, residents stay up until midnight for the privilege
of being the first town in the country to cast and count ballots and an-
nounce election results.

One of over a 1000 lakes, ponds and streams in New Hampshire which provide for a refreshing stop on warm summer days.

52.7   In Colebrook, turn left onto US 3 and ride for 26.9 miles along the Connecticut River to Groveton.

This route along the east side of the Connecticut River offers many good
views of the river and adjacent Vermont. Note the historical marker 14.8
miles south of Colebrook recounting early log drives down the river.
Just before you reach your turnoff in Groveton, you pass a covered
bridge.

In Colebrook, accommodations are available at the Colebrook
Country Club and Motel (237-5566), located on NH 26, 0.5 mile east
of its junction with US 3; and at the Northern Comfort Motel (237-4440)
located on US 3, 1.3 miles south of Colebrook.

The Wilderness Restaurant on US 3 just a few yards south of the
NH 26/US 3 junction is open all day, every day. Lambert's, a large su-
permarket, open all day, every day except Sunday when it closes at
4, is 0.3 mile north on US 3 from its junction with NH 26. South of
Colebrook you can purchase food on US 3 at Tim's Country Store (6.6
miles from Colebrook), open all day, every day; Champagne's Grocery
Store (12 miles from Colebrook); and Covill's Variety Store, both in North
Stratford and both open all day, every day. Emerson's Restaurant and
CountryStore is also open all day every day.

US 3 is the major road linking the southern half of the state with
Canada. Consequently, it carries some fast traffic and many trucks.
It is also the most hilly road on this route, with fairly consistent ups and
downs. However, the road is quite wide, the surface smooth, and the
visibility good. For 11 miles there is a good ridable shoulder. Beyond
North Stratford the shoulder disappears until the outskirts of Groveton.

79.6   In Groveton, turn left onto NH 110 and ride 26.1 miles back to Berlin.

The village of Stark, 7 miles east of Groveton on NH 110 offers one
of the most widely photographed New Hampshire scenes: the Stark
covered bridge and adjacent church, both set against a backdrop of
sheer cliffs.

In Groveton food is available at McKenzie's Dinner on US 3 just
before the downtown area (5:30–8 Mon.–Sat., 6–2 Sun.). In downtown
Groveton, S&W Market is open 8–6 Mon.–Sat., 9–1 Sun. It has a large
deli for sandwiches. P&L Mini Mart, at the junction of US 3 and NH
110 is open all day, every day. On NH 110 there are three stores open
all day, every day: Stark General Store at 6.4 miles from the junction
of US 3 and NH 110; West Milan General Store at 13.8 miles; and
Ducky's Mini Mart at 22.4 miles.

NH 110 offers a wide, smooth surface with a consistent paved
shoulder. There are some long ascents and descents; however, they
tend to be more gradual than those on US 3. Road visibility is excellent, traffic tends to be light, and the views are great. As you approach
Berlin, though, the shoulder disappears, the traffic increases, and rid-

ing conditions become distinctly urban. The last stretch of NH 110 takes you through a heavy commercial and industrial area.

104.6 At the traffic light by Andy's Market (all day Mon.–Sat., 8–9 and 1–6 Sun.) on the left, a sign points left towards NH 16. Turn left and ride one block to Madigan Street. Here, turn right and ride one block, then bear left by Jerry's Market. Continue downhill past the Berlin Police Station and through the railroad underpass to the traffic light by Dunkin' Donuts. Turn right, cycle one block, and then turn left onto NH 16. Continue past the Berlin City Bank to the traffic light by City Hall, where you turn right.

105.7 You are back at the parking lot where your trip began.

Bicycle Repair Services
Croteau and Son Bicycle Repair, Main St., Berlin (752-4963).

Guidebooks from Backcountry Publications and the Countryman Press

Written for people of all ages and experience, these highly popular and carefully prepared books feature detailed directions, notes on points of interest, sketch maps, and photographs.

For Bicyclists—
25 Bicycle Tours in Vermont, by John Freidin $7.95
20 Bicycle Tours in the Finger Lakes, by Mark Roth and Sally Walters $6.95
25 Bicycle Tours in Eastern Pennsylvania, by Dale Adams and Dale Speicher $6.95
20 Bicycle Tours In and Around New York City, by Dan Carlinsky and David Heim $6.95

About New Hampshire—
Fifty Hikes in the White Mountains, by Daniel Doan $8.95
Fifty More Hikes in New Hampshire, by Daniel Doan $8.95
Canoe Camping Vermont and New Hampshire Rivers, by Roioli Schweiker $6.95
25 Ski Tours in the White Mountains, by Daniel and Sally Ford $5.95
25 Walks in the Dartmouth-Lake Sunapee Region, by Mary L. Kibling $4.95

Other Guides—
Maine: An Explorer's Guide, by Christina Tree $9.95
Vermont: An Explorer's Guide, by Christina Tree and Peter S. Jennison $11.95
Fifty Hikes in Maine, by John Gibson $8.95
Fifty Hikes in Massachusetts, by John Brady and Brian White $8.95
Fifty Hikes in Connecticut, by Gerry and Sue Hardy $8.95
Fifty Hikes in Vermont, by Heather and Hugh Sadlier $8.95
Fifty Hikes in the Hudson Valley, by Barbara McMartin and Peter Kick $9.95
Fifty Hikes in Central New York, by William Ehling $8.95
Fifty Hikes in the Adirondacks, by Barbara McMartin $8.95

Available from bookstores, sporting goods stores, or the publisher. For a complete description of these and other guides, write The Countryman Press and Backcountry Publications, PO Box 175, Woodstock, VT 05091.